To Mom and Dad:
To building our
"heaven on earth."

Love,
Michelle ☺
XXOO

ON EARTH
AS IT IS
IN HEAVEN

ON EARTH
AS IT IS
IN HEAVEN

Jeffrey R. Holland
Patricia T. Holland

Deseret Book Company
Salt Lake City, Utah

This book is not an official publication of Brigham Young University or The Church of Jesus Christ of Latter-day Saints. The authors, and they alone, assume full responsibility for its content.

Library of Congress Cataloging-in-Publication Data

Holland, Jeffrey R., 1940–
    On earth as it is in heaven / by Jeffrey R. Holland and Patricia
T. Holland
      p. cm.
    ISBN 0-87579-186-7
    1. Spiritual life—Mormon authors. I. Holland, Patricia T.,
1942–   . II. Title.
BX8656.H655 1989
252′.09332—dc20   89-17092
                                    CIP

Printed in the United States of America

10   9   8   7   6   5   4   3   2   1

To Matt, Mary, and Duff

For creating our heaven on earth

CONTENTS

PERCEPTIONS
AND REFLECTIONS

by Patricia T. Holland

A CONVERSATION

with Jeffrey R. Holland
and Patricia T. Holland

ASSURANCES
AND AFFIRMATIONS

by Jeffrey R. Holland

PREFACE

Life here in mortality has a generous number of challenges for every one of us, and frequently we find ourselves longing for some of the peacefulness and safety of heaven. The Savior expressed not only the wish of his own heart but also that of every one of his disciples when he prayed to his Father, "Thy kingdom come, Thy will be done *on earth as it is in heaven.*" Until we can be safely home in heaven, with God and with each other, surely there is nothing higher for which we could hope than that his will and way and divine influence would be fully felt here on earth.

Such a pure and strong society will probably never be possible until Christ's millennial reign as King of kings and Lord of lords—but that is no excuse not to try to make his "kingdom come" sooner wherever that may be possible. And although heavenly circumstances may not come broadly and generally until that second advent, there are profound ways in which they can come to us personally, to our families, and to clusters of believers who live the gospel in their hearts and homes and neighborhoods.

Surely the key to any success in time or eternity is through obedience to the Son of God and his teachings, even as he

was totally obedient to the will of his Father "in all things."
This book, a collection of some of our talks and essays, is
devoted to those aspects of life near at hand in which we have
the opportunity to make God's will our will and his ways our
ways. It is devoted to the ideal of making life here "on earth"
as much as possible as it is "in heaven."

ACKNOWLEDGMENTS

We wish to thank many—especially the students of Brigham Young University—who were willing to listen to these ideas long before they came into book form. It was the privilege of a lifetime to work with such remarkable and responsive young people.

We thank a number of secretaries over the years, especially Jan Nelson and Shauna Brady, who produced untold drafts of these manuscripts. Jan Nelson also produced the final copy for this book. Special appreciation is expressed to Eleanor Knowles, executive editor of Deseret Book, who had the initial idea for this project and whose patience saw it through to publication.

PERCEPTIONS
AND REFLECTIONS

by Patricia T. Holland

Chapter 1

FILLING
THE MEASURE
OF OUR CREATION

Every element of creation has its own purpose and performance, its own divine role and mission. If our desires and works are directed toward what our heavenly parents have intended us to be, we will come to feel our part in their plan. We will recognize the "full measure of our creation," and nothing will give us more ultimate peace.

When my daughter, Mary, was just a small child, she was asked to perform a talent for a PTA contest. This is her experience exactly as she wrote it in her seven-year-old script:

"I was practicing the piano one day and it made me cry because it was bad. Then I decided to practice ballet, and it made me cry more—it was bad too. So then I decided to draw a picture because I knew I could do that good, but it was horrid. Of course it made me cry.

"Then my little three-year-old brother came up and I said, 'Duffy, what *can* I be? What can *I* be? I can't be a piano player or an artist or a ballet girl. What can I be?' He came up to me and whispered, 'You can be my sister.' "

In an important moment, those five simple words changed the perspective and comforted the heart of a very anxious child. Life became better right on the spot and, as always, tomorrow was a brighter day.

All of us face those questions about our role, our purpose, our course in life—and we face them long after we are children. I visit with enough women to know that many, perhaps most, have occasions when they feel off balance or defeated — at least temporarily. And we ask, "What will I be? When will I graduate? Whom will I marry? What is *my* future? How will I make a living? Can I make a contribution? In short, what can I be?"

Take heart if you are still asking yourself such questions because we all do. We *should* concern ourselves with our fundamental purposes in life. Surely every philosopher past and present agrees that, important as they are, food and shelter are not enough. We want to know what's next. Where is the meaning? What is my purpose?

When asking these questions, I have found it extremely reassuring to remember that one of the most important and fundamental truths taught in the scriptures and in the temple is that "every living thing shall fill the measure of its creation."

I must admit that when I first heard this directive, I thought it meant only procreation, having issue, bearing offspring. And I'm sure that is probably the most important part of its meaning. However, much of the temple ceremony is symbolic, so surely there can be multiple meanings in this statement as well. Part of the additional meaning I now see in this commandment is that every element of creation has its own purpose and performance; every one of us has been designed with a divine role and mission in mind. I believe that if our desires and works are directed toward what our heavenly parents have intended us to be, we will come to feel our part in their plan. We will recognize the "full measure of our creation," and nothing will give us more ultimate peace.

I once read a wonderful analogy of the limitations our present perspective imposes on us. The message was that in the ongoing process of creation — our creation and the creation of all that surrounds us — our heavenly parents are preparing a lovely tapestry with exquisite colors and patterns and hues. They are doing so lovingly and carefully and masterfully. And each of us is playing a part—*our* part—in the creation of that magnificent, eternal piece of art.

But in doing so we have to remember that it is very difficult for us to assess our own contribution accurately. We see the rich burgundy of a neighboring thread and think, "That's the color I want to be." Then we admire yet another's soft, restful blue or beige and think, "No, those are better colors than mine." But in all of this we don't see our work the way God sees it, nor do we realize that others are wishing they had *our* color or position or texture in the tapestry—even as we are longing for theirs.

Perhaps most important of all to remember is that through most of the creative period, we are confined to the limited view of the underside of the tapestry where things can seem particularly jumbled and muddled and unclear. If nothing really makes very much sense from that point of view, it is because we are still in process and unfinished. But our heavenly parents have the view from the top, and one day we will know what they know—that every part of the artistic whole is equal in importance and balance and beauty. They know our purpose and potential, and they have given us the perfect chance to make the perfect contribution in this divine design.

The Lord has promised us that the only qualification required to be a part of this magnificent plan is to "have desires to bring forth and establish this work." (D&C 12:7.) "Yea, whosoever will thrust in his sickle and reap, the same is called of God. Therefore, if you will ask of me you shall receive; if you will knock it shall be opened unto you." (D&C 14:4-5.)

Sometimes in our sowing and reaping and sifting, it may seem that God says "no," or "not now" or "I don't think so" when what we want for him to say, what we wish our tapestry to receive, is an affirmative "yes," or "certainly, right now" or "of course it can be yours." In my life when I have had disappointments and delays, I have lived to see that if I continue to knock with unshakable faith and persist in my patience—waiting upon the Lord and his calendar—I have discovered that the Lord's "no's" are merely preludes to an even greater "yes." I have learned that the very delays and denials we worry about most, the very differences from each other that trouble our self-esteem, are the differences and delays that are the very best for our happiness and fulfillment.

I've often wondered about the struggles that may have plagued the mind of Moses when the Lord asked him to leave his royal privileges and position in order to serve Him in abject poverty and meagerness. Contrast Moses' mission with the Lord's design for Joseph to stay in Egypt and to use his power and prestige for righteous purposes. Apparently Jeremiah was never given the blessings of marriage or children, while Jacob had the comfort and companionship of four righteous women and many children. Joshua seems to have been an incredibly confident, charismatic, take-charge kind of leader, while Moses was often reluctant, tentative, and sometimes had to ask the Lord twice for directions. Each had a crucial but very different role to play.

Furthermore, age seems to make little difference in the diversity of this tapestry. David was a mere child when he deftly dispatched Goliath, but Abraham was eighty years old when he gave us the supreme mortal example of faith and obedience. Esther had the wealth and attention of kings, giving her the opportunity to help save a nation, while Ruth was a poor, unaccepted Moabite. But it was Ruth's royal blood, ironically, that carried the lineage of the Son of God himself. The Lord uses us *because* of our unique personalities and differences rather than *in spite* of them. He needs every one of us, with all our blemishes and weaknesses and limitations.

So what *can* I be? What can *I* be? Each of us—you and I— can be what heavenly parents designed us, intended us, and help us to be. How do we fill the measure of our creation? By thrusting in a sickle and reaping with all our strength— and by rejoicing in our uniqueness and our differences. To be all that we can be, the only assignment for each of us is (1) to cherish our course and savor our own distinctiveness,

(2) to shut out conflicting voices and listen to the voice within, which is God telling us who we are and what we will be, and (3) to free ourselves from the love of profession, position, or the approval of others by remembering that what God *really* wants us to be is someone's sister, someone's brother, someone's friend.

Each of us has a purpose. And for each of us, that purpose is different; it is distinct; it is divine. God lives and loves us as we are and as we are yet to become. He will help us fill the measure of our creation.

Chapter 2

WITHIN WHISPERING DISTANCE OF HEAVEN

*Surely the prayer of faith is always heard. It is efficacious.
It is answered even if we do not understand how. That
is especially true when we are praying for others—and
never more true than when we pray for our own families
and children. Our prayers need to be more earnest and
longing, as our ancestral mothers' prayers were.*

T wo experiences were shared with me that I have combined and fictionalized to share here:

Shattered by the painfully shrill ring of her alarm clock, Jenny stumbled away from bed and toward consciousness. She got dressed in a foggy haze, which made her baggy sweatshirt and billowing jeans seem less despicable. Pulling on well-worn Adidas, she padded downstairs and silently crept outside. Beginning with a slow lope, she traced the dark outline of neighborhood trees and homes.

"I'm crazy," she said to herself. "They are all asleep—where I should be. Why am I doing this?" Then she remembered why she was doing it. "I'm worse than crazy," she thought. "I'm selfish! I shouldn't be spending this much time on myself when I have so much to do.

"I haven't lost a pound. Oh, those socks. I can't face those socks. That's why I'm here! Why do kids have to wear socks anyway? I *do* sleep better at night. Yes, running definitely helps me sleep better. Probably because no one wears socks to bed. PTA. Why do we have PTA? So we will have a meeting to go to, I suppose. I should go. Someone has to. I'm glad children don't go to PTA. That would be five more pairs of socks. I can't go to PTA tonight and still help with the kids' homework. That's ironic. I can see the headlines now – 'PTA Reviews Flunking Families. Jenny Johnson, Active PTA Member, Heads the List.'

"We've spent so much money this month. We spend so much money every month. Carolyn told me she had ten dollars' worth of groceries stolen from the glove compartment of her car.

"This new administration had better make a difference in the economy. But living off our year's supply wouldn't be so bad. It would last about a month and provide guaranteed weight loss. I wonder if Cheryl Tiegs eats wheat. Oh-oh, I don't think we have any socks in our pantry.

"Maybe I should ask to be released from Relief Society. No, I can't. I like the society and I need the relief. I hope they don't switch me to homemaking. I just couldn't bring myself to do that Samoan slap dance that Diane Davis did while waiting for her poi to cook. Maybe those women have too much time to prepare. Don't their kids wear socks?

"What kind of laundry soap does Brad's mother use? I'm so tired of that kid walking into the house looking like a Clorox ad. I'd like to throw some grape jelly right into her spin cycle. They probably discussed laundry brands in PTA the night I had the flat tire. That's the night my fourteen-year-old asked if B. F. Goodrich had done my manicure. I just smiled and ripped up a pair of his socks."

She was home again. Thirty minutes, two and one-half miles, clear, clean silence. The quiet was suddenly dispelled by an alarm buzzing upstairs and muffled pandemonium. A few minutes later, another alarm and the scampering of little feet.

"Mom, didn't you do the laundry yesterday? I'm out of underwear," said Dave. Underwear? She thought the pressure was on *socks*.

Just then Jamie yelled, "Mom, where are my socks?" Somehow the question was wonderfully reassuring. Sort of a confirmation of her home-management skills.

"Mom, who took my blue sweater?" asked Sue.

"Mom, I can't find my shoes," yelled Steve from his bedroom.

"Honey, can't you take me to work so we won't have two cars at Dave's game? I'll just have Ted drop me off."

"Ugh, cracked wheat for breakfast, Mom? I'll bet Cheryl Tiegs doesn't eat cracked wheat."

"What do you mean the only other menu is boiled, baked, or barbecued stockings? Mom, you've flipped out in your old age. You'd better stop this early morning running."

With the increasing pressures we face almost every day, it is very hard *not* to feel overwhelmed. We read of Iran and China and Russia, of high prices and hostilities and energy problems. And we read of families in trouble. We ask ourselves, "Can it be done? Can we raise a righteous family in such an increasingly difficult world?" We search for answers everywhere in psychology books and child development courses and even Erma Bombeck. We run ourselves ragged in car pools. We want straight A's and straight teeth. We panic that we're doing too much for our children and then get an Excedrin headache worrying that we're not doing enough. We even get caught in the crunch of choosing priorities between family duties and church callings—and both need our loyalty and devotion.

We feel especially anxious as our babies grow into teenagers. Sometimes it is hard to see them become independent young men and women, straining those relationships that made us feel so secure when they were in the cradle. And some in our neighborhoods experience these struggles alone, in single-parent homes. The problem isn't just this list of challenges, but that we have to face them along with the fear of graying hair, bulging tummies, and sagging energy. Occasionally we as parents would like to run away from home too—but we can't get the keys to the car.

Humor aside, we know how serious our task is. We are, after all, the generation raised on the admonition, "No other success in life can compensate for failure in the home." The weight of that statement oftentimes seems more than we can bear. But I've decided that anything very important is weighty and difficult. Perhaps the Lord designed it that way so we would cherish and retain and magnify treasures that matter the most. Like the seeker in the parable, we too must be willing to go and sell all that we have for those pearls of great price. Our families, along with our testimonies and loyalty to the Lord, are the most prized of all such pearls. I think you'll agree they are worth some agony and anxiety. To have it all go along easily might mislead us in time and leave us ill-prepared for eternity.

I also believe that with the task is given the talent. Like Nephi, I do not believe God will ask us to do this most important thing without preparing the way for us to accomplish it. These are his children too, and we must never forget that fact in joy or sorrow. We have additional parental help through the veil. We are able to say with the angels, "Is any thing too hard for the Lord?" (Genesis 18:14.) I have taken great comfort in that scripture over the years. It is a family-oriented scripture. It is the scripture at the heart of everything we now call the seed of Abraham, Isaac, and Jacob.

In our early married life it appeared as if I too, like Sarah, would be barren. My doctor told us that there was a good chance we would have no children. But in my heart I felt otherwise, and I remembered Sarah. Is anything too hard for the Lord? No, not if their names are Matthew, Mary Alice, and David. Is it too hard to conceive them or bear them or nurse them or comfort them or teach them or clothe them or wait up for them or be patient with them or cry over them or love them? No, not if these are God's children as well as ours. Not if we remember those maternal stirrings that are,

11

I suppose, the strongest natural affections in the world. President David O. McKay said once that the nearest thing to Christ's love for mankind was a mother's love for her child. Everything I have felt since June 7, 1966, tells me he was right.

When troubles come—and they will; when challenges mount—and they will; when evil abounds and we fear for our children's lives, we can think of the covenant and promise given to Abraham, and especially think of Sarah. And with the angels we can repeat the question, "Is anything too hard for the Lord?"

If you think circumstances in your life are not ideal, take heart. I'm beginning to wonder if circumstances ever are ideal. Let me use my own life as an example.

Because of various educational and professional assignments that have come to us, we have moved some fifteen times in our marriage. When the children started to come, those moves were an increasing concern to me. I worried about their adjusting and settling in and finding friends. Their emotional safety through our very busy lives has caused me a great deal of concern.

When we were in graduate school with two small children, the student housing we lived in was on the edge of the black community, in New Haven, Connecticut. Almost all the other student residents in that area either put their children in private schools or jumped district boundaries. Because we could not afford a private school and felt it dishonest to jump boundaries, Matt was literally the only white boy in his kindergarten class and one of two white children in the entire school.

I can still remember the tears and the terror. This was my firstborn, the treasure of my life. He was the boy I'd practiced all my child development courses on. This was the child I had taught to read before he was three. This was the child I was certain was destined to become one of the legendary greats of western civilization. How could his educational beginnings, his first stirrings from the warmth and protection of the nest, be so startling—so much to adjust to? But I remembered then and remember now something George Bernard Shaw once said: "People are always blaming their circumstances for what they are. I don't believe in circumstances. The people who get on in this world are the people who get up and look for the circumstances they want, and, if they can't find them, make them." (*Mrs. Warren's Profession,* act 2.)

Clinging to the hope that maybe this was one of those opportunities for growth, and fighting to control my fears, I threw myself into the school PTA. I also volunteered to provide music training at the school once a week. Well, that was one year that seems so long ago. A great deal happened then and since, but suffice it to say that we are greatly blessed that our whole family has been able to appreciate a broader racial and cultural world. And it goes without saying that Matt has become the most culturally and racially sensitive of all our children.

Another example from the same period. We were very busy during those years. We were living in the mission field, which required that our service to our ward be greater than usual. I was called to serve as Relief Society president, Sunday School chorister, and Laurel adviser. I also worried that these demands were robbing me of close mother-child nurturing with my infant daughter. For years afterward I believed that every moment of colic or croup in her life somehow stemmed from that period. My guilt, real or imagined, was immense.

With time and perspective I can see now that because of my concerns I probably worked overtime to compensate for all losses. This daughter has now developed into a young woman with great self-confidence. She is very much at home with herself and with me. Ours is one of the most rewarding mother-daughter relationships I know of.

When we moved to Provo, Utah, we faced another very demanding time in our lives. The role of a university president's wife can be a full-time job with a generous amount of overtime. And with our home situated on the campus, my children would not have friends living next door. They would

13

have students pointing them out—nicely but still conspicuously—and reminding them that they were "the president's
children." In a great many ways it was a difficult time, but it
carried with it its own special blessings and opportunities.
We determined to make it a very rich and rewarding experience, and I believe we did.

So it seems to me that Shaw was right. You don't simply
yield to circumstances; you shape and use them for your own
best purposes. Circumstances are seldom ideal, but our ideals
can prevail, especially where they affect home and children.

Of the atmosphere surrounding his childhood home,
President Spencer W. Kimball wrote: "My own wonderful
mother's journal records a lifetime of being grateful for the
opportunity to serve, and of feeling regretful only that she
couldn't do more. I smiled when I recently read one entry,
dated January 16, 1900. She was serving as first counselor in
the Relief Society presidency in Thatcher, Arizona, and the
presidency went to a sister's home where caring for a sick
baby had kept the mother from doing her sewing. Mother
took her own sewing machine, a picnic lunch, her baby, and
a high chair, and they began work. She wrote that night that
they had 'made four aprons, four pairs of pants and started
a shirt for one of the boys.' They had to stop at four o'clock
to go to a funeral, so they 'did not get any more than that
done.' I would have been impressed by such an achievement,
rather than thinking, 'Well, that's not much.' " President Kimball then went on to say, "That's the kind of home into which
I was born, one conducted by a woman who breathed service
in all her actions." (*Woman* [Salt Lake City: Deseret Book,
1979], pp. 1-2.)

Did you know that President Kimball's mother died when
he was only eleven, while his father was presiding over a
stake that stretched from St. Johns, Arizona, to El Paso, Texas?

Did you know that President McKay was only eight years
old when he became the man of the house? His father was
called on a mission to Great Britain, two older sisters had just

recently died, and his mother was expecting another baby. Young David's father felt he simply could not leave under those circumstances, but his wife stated unequivocally that he would go. She said, "Little David and I will manage this household very nicely."

Did you know that President Heber J. Grant's father died when Heber was only eight days old? Heber's bishop didn't think the young boy would ever amount to anything because he played baseball too much. But his mother knew what only mothers know, and she molded the future of a young prophet.

Did you know that President Joseph Fielding Smith was born while his father, Joseph F. Smith, was serving as a member of the Quorum of the Twelve? And that Joseph Fielding was only four years old when his father became a member of the First Presidency?

Did you know that President Joseph F. Smith was born during those terrible persecutions of the Latter-day Saints in Missouri? And that when he was only five years old, he stood over the coffins of his father, Hyrum Smith, and his uncle, the Prophet Joseph Smith, as they lay in state in the Mansion House in Nauvoo, Illinois, after they had been cruelly murdered by a mob at Carthage Jail? You may remember that young Joseph and his mother faced incredible hardships as they fought their way west. What you may not remember is that soon after they arrived in Utah, Mary Fielding Smith died, leaving young Joseph an orphan. But she had done what no one else could do. Her son would later write of her, "Oh my God, how I love and cherish true motherhood! Nothing beneath the celestial kingdom can surpass my deathless love for the sweet, true, noble soul who gave me my birth . . . my own, own mother! She was good! She was pure! She was indeed a Saint! A royal daughter of God. To her I owe my very existence as also my success in life." (Don Cecil Corbett, *Mary Fielding Smith, Daughter of Britain* [Salt Lake City: Deseret Book, 1966], p. 268.)

Did you know that Brigham Young spent his very early

years helping his father clear timber off new land and cultivate the ground? He remembered logging and driving teams summer and winter, half clad and with insufficient food until his "stomach would ache." When he was fourteen years old, his mother died, leaving the numerous domestic responsibilities to the father and the children.

When we feel the desire to murmur, when we ask for more means, or more time, or more psychology, or more energy, or even if we wish we just didn't have to do it alone, let's pause and ask one more time, "Is anything too hard for the Lord?" If a daughter misses one segment in ballet training, perhaps the sun will still rise tomorrow.

Had Mary Fielding Smith heard our contemporary complaints while administering to her stricken ox and raising it from the dead, she might have smiled just a little at our dismay over such things as the price of gasoline. If we seem to lack something found in the homes of our prophets, maybe what we've suffered is not too much affliction but too little. Could it be that the answers are only to be found on our knees, as our prophets were required to do, while waiting patiently upon the Lord?

We don't live in the same world with the same challenges that our grandmothers or great-grandmothers faced. As the world changes, our challenges seem to be newer and more complex, if not necessarily more heartrending. However, I am convinced that we will fail in our responsibilities—as they would have failed in theirs—if we don't exert the same kind of faith they had. An early-morning run might help us face a laundry crisis, but Christian commandments are necessary for real salvation, both emotional and eternal. Our prayers need to be more earnest and longing, as were the prayers of our ancestral mothers, if we are to obtain the salvation for which we seek.

Now perhaps you are saying, "But I am praying now. I am faithfully on my knees, but the answers still don't come." All I can say is that the Lord's counsel seems to be to ask more often, however faithfully you are now praying. Are our hands blotchy, as President Kimball said, from knocking at heaven's door? Do we "labor in the spirit" in any sense that is really labor? Women appreciate that word *labor* in a way that no man ever can. Do we labor spiritually to deliver our children from evil to the degree that we labored to bring them into the world? Is that fair to ask? But is it faithful not to ask?

"Alma labored much in the spirit, wrestling with God in mighty prayer, that he would pour out his Spirit upon the people." (Alma 8:10.) We must do at least as much to call down the Spirit into our homes and into the lives of our children. Indeed, this very son, Alma, is an excellent example of a child who was not only brought to repentance of his former sins but who was also raised up to become one of the Nephites' greatest prophets. All of this was the result of the faith and prayers of a righteous father.

When an angel appeared to Alma the younger and the sons of Mosiah, he said: "The Lord hath heard the prayers of his people, and also the prayers of his servant, Alma, who is thy father; for he has prayed with much faith concerning thee; . . . therefore, for this purpose have I come to convince thee of the power and authority of God, that the prayers of his servants might be answered according to their faith." (Mosiah 27:14.)

I believe with all my heart that the prayer of faith is heard, is efficacious, is answered. I especially believe that to be true when we pray for others—and never more true than when we pray for our own families and children.

Faithful scripture study seems another oft-cited yet overlooked habit, but I have personally taken great comfort in this comment from President Kimball. He said of his beloved wife, Camilla, "I think of the spirit of revelation that my own dear wife invites into our home because of the hours she has spent every year of our married life in studying the scriptures, so that she can be prepared to teach the principles of the gospel." (*Woman,* p. 1.)

17

Where should we turn when we hear so many confusing voices trying to define our role as mothers in today's world? Are we studying the illuminating truths of the past, the words for which prophets have died and angels have flown? Can we with impunity disregard them as a vast repository of God's clearest instructions, and still cry that he has left us alone in a wicked, worrisome world? We should be studying the scriptures as ancient Israel did, both day and night. Then our problems and perplexities will be aided, as President Kimball noted, by "the spirit of revelation."

And so, with simple, traditional, tried-and-true principles, such as earnest prayer, serious scriptural study, devoted fasting, compassionate service, and patient forbearance, the blessings of heaven distill upon us even to include the personal manifestations of the Son of God himself.

President Harold B. Lee promised, "If we will live worthy, then the Lord will guide us—by personal appearance, or by His actual voice, or by His voice coming into our mind, or by impressions upon our heart and our soul." (*Stand Ye in Holy Places* [Salt Lake City: Deseret Book, 1974], p. 144.)

And President David O. McKay said, "Pure hearts in a pure home are always in whispering distance of heaven." (Dean Zimmerman, comp., *Sentence Sermons* [Salt Lake City: Deseret Book, 1978], p. 91.)

I was reared in a pure home by people with pure hearts, and for me that has made all the difference. When my mother was carrying me, my parents lived in a tent while my father sought work during World War II. Shortly after I was conceived, my mother became ill and threatened to miscarry. The doctor, whose office was sixty miles away, told her that if she were to keep the baby, she must go to bed and stay the entire nine months. She, without complaining, tells of the hardship of trying to keep two small, active boys entertained in a tent, which was extremely hot in the summer months and cold in the winter, while she lay flat on her back in bed. All of her friends and neighbors counseled her to get up and lose the baby naturally—because it would probably be deformed anyway. But my mother, who has taught me something about prayer, personal sacrifice, endurance, and deep faith, persevered.

I thank my mother for her devotion to and reverence for life. Much of what I feel about motherhood and family I inherited from this saintly woman. In more than the clichéd standard way, I acknowledge that I owe my life to her. She lives within whispering distance of heaven.

Yes, there are answers to our anxieties. Some of them may come painfully and some of them may come very, very slowly. But I believe with all my heart that they will come if we will believe and follow our Lord Jesus Christ.

Chapter 3

EVERYTHING TO DO
WITH THE HEART

*Every child has to practice on his mother and, in an
important way, every mother has to practice on her child.
That is God's way for parent and child to work out their
salvation. But it helps us to always remember that these
are God's children as well as our own, and that when
we need help, we can reach through the veil to get it.*

W hen a four-year-old was asked recently why her
baby brother was crying, she looked at the baby,
thought for a moment, and then said, "Well, if you
had no hair, no teeth, and your legs were wobbly, you would
cry too."

We all come into the world crying—and a little bit wobbly.
For parents to take a newborn infant, who is then only a
bundle of potentialities, and love and guide and develop that
child until a fully functional human being emerges is the
grandest miracle of science and the greatest of all arts.

When the Lord created parents, he created something
breathtakingly close to what he is. We who have borne children innately know that this is the highest of callings, the
holiest of assignments—and that is why the slightest failure
can cause us crippling despair.

Even with our best intentions and our most heartfelt efforts, some of us find our children not turning out the way
we'd like. They are sometimes very difficult to communicate
with. They might be struggling in school or emotionally dis-

tressed or openly rebellious or painfully shy. There are lots of reasons why they may still be wobbling a bit.

And it seems that even if our children are not having problems, a nagging uneasiness keeps us wondering how we can keep them off such painful paths. At odd moments we find ourselves thinking, "Am I doing a good job? Are they going to make it? Should I spank them or should I reason with them? Should I control them or should I just ignore them?" Reality has a way of making the best of us feel shaky as parents.

I just reread this recently from my journal, written when I was a young and a very anxious mother:

"I continually pray that I will never do anything to injure my children emotionally. If I ever do cause them to hurt in any way, I pray they will know I did it unwittingly. I cry often inside for things I may have said and done thoughtlessly, and I pray not to repeat these transgressions. I pray that I haven't done anything to damage my dream of what I want these children to become. I hunger for help and a guide—particularly when I feel that I have failed them."

Rereading that after all these years makes me feel my children are turning out surprisingly well for having had such a basket case for a mother. And I share it because what I want most of all to convey is that I am one with you—a parent, carrying a bundle of guilt for past mistakes, shaky confidence for the present, and fear of future failing. Above all, I want every parent to have hope.

Inasmuch as almost none of us is a professional in child development, you can imagine why I was so encouraged to hear this from one who is. A faculty member at Brigham Young University said to me one day, "Pat, parenting has almost nothing to do with training. It has everything to do with your heart." When I asked him to explain further, he said, "Often parents feel the reason they do not communicate with their children is that they are not skillful enough. Communication is not nearly so much a matter of skill as it is of attitude. When our attitude is one of brokenheartedness and humility, of love and interest in our children's welfare, then *that* cultivates communication. Our children recognize that effort on our part. On the other hand, when we are impatient, hostile, or resentful, it doesn't matter what words we choose or how we try to camouflage our feelings. That attitude will be felt by their discerning hearts."

Jacob in the Book of Mormon said we must all come down in the depths of humility and consider ourselves fools before God if we would have him open the gate of heaven to us. (2 Nephi 9:42.)

That humility, including our ability to admit our mistakes, seems to be fundamental both for receiving divine help and for earning our children's respect.

My daughter is a musically talented young woman. For many years I felt that this talent would not be developed unless I loomed over her at the piano and insistently supervised her practice like a Simon Legree. One day, sometime in her early teens, I realized that my attitude, probably once useful, was now visibly affecting our relationship. Torn between a fear that she would not fully develop a God-given talent and the reality of an increasingly strained relationship over that very issue, I did what I had seen my own mother do when faced with a serious challenge. I sequestered myself in my secret place and poured out my soul in prayer, seeking the only wisdom that could help me keep that communication open—the kind of wisdom and help that comes from the tongues of angels. Upon arising from my knees, I knew what action I must take.

Because it was just three days before Christmas, I gave to Mary as a personal gift an apron from which I had conspicuously cut the apron strings. In a tiny pocket on the apron I tucked a note that read: "Dear Mary, I'm sorry for the conflict I have caused by acting like a federal marshal at the piano. I must have looked foolish there—just you and me and my six-shooters. Forgive me. You are becoming a young woman in your own right. I have only worried that you would not feel as fully confident and fulfilled as a woman if you left your talent unfinished. I love you. Mom."

Later that day she sought me out, and, in a quiet corner of our home, she said, "Mother, I know you want what's best for me, and I have known that all my life. But if I'm ever going to play the piano well, *I'm* the one who has to do the practicing, not you." Then she threw her arms around me and, with tears in her eyes, said, "I've been wondering how to teach you that—and somehow you figured it out on your own."

Now, by her own choice, she has gone on to even more disciplined musical development. And I am always nearby to encourage her.

As Mary and I reminisced about this experience a few years later, she confided in me that my willingness to say "I'm sorry, I've made a mistake, please forgive me" gave her a great sense of self-worth, because it said to her that she was worthy enough for a parental apology, that sometimes children can be right. I wonder if personal revelation ever comes without counting ourselves as fools before God? I wonder if reaching and teaching our children requires becoming more childlike ourselves? Shouldn't we share our deepest fears and pain with them, as well as our highest hopes and joys, instead of simply trying to lecture and dominate and reprove them again and again?

When our youngest son, Duffy, was eleven years old and a would-be linebacker, for three days in a row he leaped from some hidden corner of our home to throw a body block on me, Super-Bowl-style. The last time he did this, in my effort to avoid the blitz, I fell on the floor and knocked over the lamp and found my right elbow wedged up somewhere near my eyebrow. I completely lost my patience, and I scolded him dearly for making me his tackling dummy.

His response melted my heart when he said, with tears rolling down both cheeks, "But, Mom, you're the best friend a guy could have. I thought this was as much fun for you as it was for me." Then he added, "For a long time now I've planned what I will say in my first interview as a Heisman Trophy winner. When they ask me how I got to be so great, I'll tell them, 'I practiced on my mother!' "

Every child has to practice on his mother and, in a more important way, every mother has to practice on her child. That is God's way for parent and child to work out their salvation. I mentioned earlier that we all come into the world crying. Considering all the humbling purposes of life, perhaps it is understandable that we will continue to shed a tear or two from time to time. But it helps us to remember always that these are God's children as well as ours. And above all, it should give us a perfect brightness of hope to know that when we need help, we can go through the veil to get it.

I testify that God will never give up on us in this heavenly designed experience, and we must never give up on our children — or on ourselves.

Chapter 4

THE FRUITS OF PEACE

The love of God and one's neighbor is the only door out of the dungeon of the self. The region of a woman's life is a spiritual region. God, her neighbors, and her family and friends—this is the wide world in which alone her spirit can find room to grow.

T he Lord has said, "I am the vine, ye are the branches: He that abideth in me, and I in him, the same bringeth forth much fruit: for without me ye can do nothing." (John 15:5.) He also said, through Paul, "The fruit of the Spirit is love, joy, peace." (Galatians 5:22.) It is about the fruit of our effort that I wish to speak—the fruit of love and joy, which is ultimately the fruit of peace. It is a harvest that can come only in the Lord's way. Its roots are deep in the gospel of Jesus Christ.

It seems tragic to me that women are often their own worst enemies when they ought to be allies, nurturing and building each other. We all know how much a man's opinion of us can mean, but I believe our self-worth as women is often reflected to us in the eyes of other women. When other women respect us, we respect ourselves. It is often only when other women find us pleasant and worthy that we find ourselves pleasant and worthy. If we have this effect on each other, why aren't we more generous and loving with one another?

I've thought long and often about this. I have finally come to suspect that part of the problem is the heart. We are afraid—

afraid to reach out, afraid to reach up, afraid to trust and be trusted, especially with and by other women. In short, we don't love enough. We don't exercise to full capacity the greatest gift and power God gave to women.

Dr. Gerald G. Jampolsky, a psychiatrist at the University of California, tells us that love is an innate characteristic. It is already there. But too often it becomes clouded over with fear, which, through life's experiences, we've conjured up ourselves. He says, "When you feel love for all, not just those you choose, but all those [with] whom you come in contact — you experience peace. When you feel fear with anyone you come in contact with, you want to defend yourselves and attack others and there comes the conflict." (*Love Is Letting Go of Fear* [New York: Bantam Books, 1981], p. 2.)

Obviously, we have a choice. If Dr. Jampolsky is right, we can choose love and experience peace, or choose fear and experience conflict. Quoting again from Dr. Jampolsky, "In order to experience peace instead of conflict, it is necessary to shift our perception. Instead of seeing others as attacking us, we can see them as fearful. We are always experiencing love or fear. Fear is really a call for help and therefore a request for love. It is apparent then that in order to experience peace we do have a choice in determining the way we perceive things."

Moroni made the same observation. He maintained that he was able to overcome fear because he was full of charity, which is everlasting love: "Behold, I speak with boldness, having authority from God; and I fear not what man can do; for perfect love casteth out all fear." (Moroni 8:16.)

If the fear of other women or of men causes our conflict, and unconditional love for them brings us the valued peace we so desire, then shouldn't the whole pursuit of our lives be to extend love everywhere and to everyone? Doesn't it make you want to put every ounce of energy you have into the practice and pursuit of perfect love?

But just desiring to love doesn't necessarily make it happen. Those who try hardest will be most aware of falling short. I encourage you not to be discouraged. I have on occasion prayed to love someone better only to find a great division come between us temporarily—but from which eventually, and with much work, grows a deeper, more tender love. Erich Fromm has written, "Because one does not see that love is an activity, a power of the soul, one believes that all that is necessary to find is the right object—and that everything goes by itself afterward. This attitude can be compared to that of a man who wants to paint but who, instead of learning the art, claims that he has just to wait for the right object, and that he will paint beautifully when he finds it." (Quoted in *Secrets to Share*, sel. Lois Daniel [New York: Hallmark, 1971], p. 59.) Love is like any other talent, art, skill, or virtue. It takes practice, perspiration, knowledge, and plenty of time. Willingness does not imply mastery, but it does mean we are willing to try.

In my younger years, I nurtured tender dreams of becoming an accomplished pianist. Reaching such a goal requires daily exercises, performances, recitals, trial and error, trying again and again for many years. We might view the pursuit of lasting love and perfect peace in exactly the same way—except that the Lord tells us that charity is the greatest of all talents, gifts, and virtues. But, as Mormon taught, "If ye have not charity, ye are nothing." (Moroni 7:46.) That scripture contains a classic, crucial observation about self-worth. To be anybody, we must love everybody.

Now, getting back to the "practice" of love, I would like to suggest three basic exercises to develop this gift.

Exercise number one is to forgive. Forgiveness is the key to peace in personal relationships. If we can somehow wipe the slate clean and see everyone as blameless, we will begin to see ourselves as blameless. Remember Dr. Jampolsky's observation about fear and love. It may help us to forgive others their offenses and attacks against us if we can see that they were operating out of fear and not malice.

27

At one time I worked with another woman in the presidency of an organization in one of the many wards we have lived in. She often teasingly belittled me, but because it was done in jest, she felt she could get away with it. However, it became a great source of hurt and irritation to me. While trying to practice this concept of forgiveness, I realized that every time I received a jab in jest, it was because of an inadequacy this sister felt in herself. I really believe that she was a frightened woman. In the privacy of her own life and out of earshot or eyesight from me, she was so busy nursing her own hurt that she simply was not able to consider anyone else's. In some unfortunate way, I believe she felt she had so little to give that any compliment or virtue extended to another would somehow demean her. She needed my love, and I was foolish to take offense.

President Spencer W. Kimball counseled that as we try to overlook whatever others have done to us, we will begin to let go of all that has been hard to forgive in ourselves. We will feel peace and wholeness, and we will remember that the Lord suffered for our sins so we could experience at-one-ment with him, with our neighbors, and, very importantly, within ourselves. (See *Faith Precedes the Miracle* [Salt Lake City: Deseret Book, 1972], pp. 190-96.)

Exercise number two is to accept others unconditionally. What we want most of all is the approval, praise, and unconditional love of others. Can we give less than what we desire for ourselves?

One day my feelings had been deeply hurt by a close neighbor. Feeling what I was sure at the time was deserved self-pity, I went to my room and poured out my broken heart in prayer. I remember specifically saying, "Dear Father in heaven, please help me to find a friend whom I can trust, one whom I know I'll love." He did bless me—he gave me, for a moment, the uncluttered insight that can come only by the Spirit. He helped me to see that I was praying for a perfect friend, while he had generously surrounded me with friends whose weaknesses were like my own.

A good relationship is not one in which perfection reigns; rather, it is one in which a healthy perspective simply overlooks the faults of others.

Here is a very specific way to practice this exercise. For one day, make a note each time you critically evaluate someone. This doesn't have to be a spoken criticism (though this, too, should be considered), but it is important to note each time you pass even unspoken judgment. Judgments might be passed against yourself, your own children, your husband, a neighbor, or a friend. Then the next day, see if you can go the entire day without being critical or petty toward anyone.

This little exercise might surprise you. My husband will verify that I conscientiously work at never speaking ill of anyone. It is a virtue I earnestly seek, and I see it as fundamental to true Christianity. When I undertook this little exercise, therefore, it amazed me to realize how often I did pass judgment, at least mentally. I was even more amazed to note how incredibly good I felt about myself when I was able to get through a whole day keeping that tendency in check. Remember that whatever you toss out mentally or verbally comes back to you according to God's plan of compensation: "For with what judgment ye judge, ye shall be judged: and with what measure ye mete, it shall be measured to you again." (Matthew 7:2.) A critical, petty, or vicious remark is simply an attack on our own self-worth. On the other hand, if our minds are constantly seeing good in others, that, too, will return, and we will truly feel good about ourselves.

Exercise number three is to give without any thought of getting. Now, I don't mean we should be martyrs in any way. But to be totally accepting of others, we must accept the fact that they cannot satisfy all of our desires. People can only be what they are—at least for the present. They can give only what they have at that moment to give. They may not have had as much knowledge of or practice at love as we have had. Yet when we want them to give us something they cannot give, we feel frustrated, angry, despondent, ill, rejected, or attacked.

For a long period in my life, there was a women I admired very much whose unconditional love I would have cherished. I tried everything I knew to win her love, but nothing seemed to work. Then I read one day that the first principle of good mental health is to accept that which cannot be changed. I finally understood that this woman did love as much as she was able—and suddenly our entire relationship changed. It was more formal and restrained than I would have liked, but it was a relationship. If it had continued with my demanding more than she could give, it would surely have withered and died. In a sense, I had nurtured that particular plant in too small a pot. So I repotted it in a container more suitable to its size, gave it more room for growth, and it began to flourish. I could see that the fruit in this relationship was well worth some one-way nourishing, and I'm content now to wait until she is ready to give.

I want you to know that when I have practiced these exercises effectively, it has produced a miracle.

I used to be very shy. It was quite painful for me to make a move every two years or so as we were pursuing my husband's career. Each new move was filled with fear. Would I be accepted? Would we live where people were more qualified than I? Would we live in a neighborhood where people could give their children more opportunities? With several of our first moves, we lived in the new area only a few months (and I was still striving to establish a new identity) when I was called to serve as the ward Relief Society president. God must have smiled as he saw that it took several repetitions of this same experience before I was able to see that at the precise moment I began to practice my love on the sisters and their families in these wards, I immediately lost all fear. It is my personal witness that if, instead of seeing life through the vainly colored lens of getting, we would practice changing our focus to unrestricted giving, we would forget about fear and conflict and begin to know real and lasting peace.

Those are my three exercises. Yet, even as I encourage you to practice, you must know that the demands of the real contest can be staggering. The suggestions I offer for minor conflicts, hurt, or irritations may not help much if someone took the life of your child, or stole the affections of your husband, or intentionally hurt you in some other unjust way.

In light of those greater needs, I bear this witness: There is in this world much that can be accomplished only with the help of God. If he tells us to love, he will give us the power to do so.

Perhaps you have read Corrie Ten Boom's book *The Hiding Place*. Have any of us been asked to experience the intensity of such injustices as she describes? Have we experienced the numbing fear of war, of prison camps, of the death of family and friends? Following is an excerpt from her book in which she relates an experience just as the war has ended. She has been released from prison camps, and her only desire is to teach her people that the way to rebuild is through love. Then she faces a startling and unexpected challenge:

"It was at a church service in Munich that I saw him, the former S.S. man who had stood guard at the shower room door in the processing center at Ravensbruck. He was the first of our actual jailers that I had seen since that time. And suddenly it was all there—the roomful of mocking men, the heaps of our clothing, Betsie's pain-blanched face.

"He came up to me as the church was emptying, beaming and bowing. 'How grateful I am for your message, Fraulein,' he said. 'To think that, as you say, He washed my sins away!'

"His hand was thrust out to shake mine. And I, who had preached so often to the people in Bloemendaal the need to forgive, kept my hand at my side.

"Even as the angry, vengeful thoughts boiled through me, I saw the sin of them. Jesus Christ had died for this man;

was I going to ask for more? Lord Jesus, I prayed, forgive me and help me to forgive him.

"I tried to smile, I struggled to raise my hand. I could not. I felt nothing, not the slightest spark of warmth or charity. And so again I breathed a silent prayer. Jesus, I cannot forgive him. Give me Your forgiveness.

"As I took his hand the most incredible thing happened. From my shoulder along my arm and through my hand a current seemed to pass from me to him, while into my heart sprang a love for this stranger that almost overwhelmed me.

"And so I discovered that it is not on our forgiveness any more than on our goodness that the world's healing hinges, but on His. When He tells us to love our enemies, He gives, along with the command, the love itself." (*The Hiding Place* [New York: Bantam Books, 1974], p. 238.)

Moroni taught the same principle: "Wherefore, my beloved brethren, pray unto the Father with all the energy of heart, that ye may be filled with this love, which he hath bestowed upon all who are true followers of his Son, Jesus Christ." (Moroni 7:48.)

This perfect love, the kind that brings real peace, is *bestowed*. It is a gift given from our Father in heaven in answer to the prayer of faith. We often will have no ability or power beyond our ability to plead for God's help.

May I conclude by describing a sisterly relationship that may be the most sacred in all of scripture. Never before or since have two women — friends, neighbors, and in the same family circle — been chosen to bear such responsibilities. Their roots had to be deep, for the fruit of their loins would be the fruit of peace for an entire world.

I have always been touched that in her moment of greatest need, her singular time of confusion and wonder and awe, Mary went to another woman. She knew she could go to Elisabeth. I have also been touched that age was no factor here; in God's love there is no generation gap. Mary was very young — probably in her mid-teens at most — and Elisabeth was well beyond her childbearing years. The scripture says she was "well stricken" in years. (Luke 1:7.) Yet these two women came together, greeting one another in a bond that only women can know. Indeed, it was their very womanhood that God used for his holiest of purposes. And in the special roles they were destined to play, these two beloved women – representing both personally and dispensationally the old and the new – sang to each other even as the babe in the womb of one leapt in recognition of the divinity of the other.

Elisabeth was not petty or fearful or envious. Her son would not have the fame or role or divinity that had been bestowed on Mary's child; but her only feelings were of love and devotion. To this young, bewildered kinswoman she said only, "Blessed art *thou* among women, and blessed is the fruit of *thy* womb. And whence is this to *me,* that the mother of my Lord should come to *me?*" (Luke 1:42-43. Italics added.)

Mary also knew that humility and selflessness are the watchwords. She knew that when she said to the Angel Gabriel, "Be it unto me according to *thy* word." (Luke 1:38. Italics added.) And here to Elisabeth she sang, "My soul doth magnify the Lord. . . . He hath scattered the proud in the imagination of their hearts." (Luke 1:46, 51.)

This exchange between these two different yet similar women seems to me the essence of love and peace and purity. Surely the challenge for our day is to be equally pure in our womanhood. When we pollute the powerful potential for love with our pettiness and our fears, then disease replaces emotional health, and despondency replaces peace.

As women, we have the choice and privilege to connect ourselves to God in a way whereby we draw his nourishing love down to our very roots. Such peace and power can then be extended to others. Like Mary, whose sweet joy and terrible burden could not be self-contained, each of us could find an Elisabeth to turn to if we would live for that relationship.

Like the cycles of trees and roots and branches, a woman's love can be one eternal round. When we love the Lord, we love each other; and when we love each other, we love ourselves. Then the harvest is indeed the fruit of peace.

With only a shift in his pronouns, I share this concluding thought from George MacDonald:

"This love of [God and] one's neighbor is the only door out of the dungeon of self. To have herself, to know herself, to enjoy herself, this she calls life; whereas, if she would forget herself, tenfold would be her life in God and her neighbors. The region of woman's life is a spiritual region. God, her friends, her neighbors, her sisters all, is the wide world in which alone her spirit can find room. Herself is her dungeon.

"[In giving to others never] shall a woman lose the consciousness of [her own] well-being. Far deeper and more complete, God and her neighbor will flash it back upon her—pure as life. No more will she agonize to generate it in the light of her own decadence. For she shall know the glory of her own being in the light of God and of her sisters." (George MacDonald, *Creation in Christ* [Wheaton, Ill.: Harold Shaw, 1976], p. 304.)

Chapter 5

THE COMFORT
WHEREWITH WE
ARE COMFORTED

Sometimes when we are the loneliest or when we feel the greatest hurt is precisely the time when we feel God is not there, the very time when we feel utterly abandoned by him. But our willingness to make that leap of faith toward his embrace—when we are least certain of his presence—could be the most important act of our lives.

T he things that matter most to me, the things I would most want to exemplify, are the quieter, less visible aspects of life. The kinds of virtues I wish to stand for, if I am able, are personal, not professional. I would like to be known as a wife, a mother, and a friend—a personal, caring friend. I would hope these modest goals can qualify one as an exemplary woman. I was given these values by my beloved parents—parents who, along with my dear mother-in-law, my husband, and my children, have given me days and nights of private support far from the spotlight of public appearance and applause. They have always been beautiful examples of deep love and quiet service.

In order to speak about service, I must begin where all things begin: with God. Many of us want to serve but we do not—or feel we cannot—either because we are consumed with our own problems or because we simply lack the confidence to reach out. All of us want to be more charitable, more generous, and more loving. We have been told over and over again that a true sense of self-worth comes from service—that to find your life you must lose it. Yet too often something blocks our ability and our efforts.

It is to those who desire to serve, but who feel they lack the courage, strength, or ability, that I wish to speak. To do so I need to speak about God.

While praying one evening about how to address this perplexing problem, I felt that I was led directly to the words of Paul. In a little known and seldom quoted line from 2 Corinthians, I read: "Blessed be God, even the Father of our Lord Jesus Christ, the Father of mercies, and the God of all comfort; who comforteth us in all our tribulation, that we may be able to comfort them which are in trouble, by the comfort wherewith we are comforted of God." (2 Corinthians 1:3.)

I cannot express the power and peace I felt when I read that scripture. What a world of meaning and instruction condensed into those simple lines! Concentrate with me for a moment on the first promise—that God is the God of all comfort—and we will consider the second half of the verse later. Inasmuch as all of us need comfort at so many different moments every day of our lives, it is wonderfully reassuring that *our* God, *our* Father, "is the God of *all* comfort." That phrase "of all comfort" means to me not only that there is no *greater* source available for solace and strength, but that technically speaking there is no *other* source.

After several years on the Brigham Young University campus with so many opportunities to speak with hundreds of students, I have come to realize that virtually every one of us carries around burdens and fears that wear us down and greatly oppress us. I think it is obvious that the emotional burdens, the spiritual struggles, I have seen people carry are far more burdensome and frightening than the prospects of any physical limitations we may face in life. According to a recent study of mental health in America, plain old-fashioned worry is one of the few emotional problems that is on the increase, for reasons that are not altogether clear to physicians and behavioral scientists. Dr. Claire Weekes, in trying to discover a pattern for such emotional and spiritual worry, said, "The basic problem is fear. Guilt opens the door to fear. Anxiety, worry, dread, conflict, even sorrow are only variants of fear in different guises." (*Hope and Help for Your Nerves* [New York: Hawthorn Books, 1969], p. 21.)

It is in response to these very modern challenges that God comes to us as "the Father of mercies, and the God of all comfort." What a reassurance and reward just to know that such all-encompassing help is available to us in our anxious times. No wonder we lovingly call him Father.

But do we really picture an actual father when we pray? Do we think of him — do we *truly* think of Him — as our Father? Do we spend any time on our knees trying to picture the being to whom we pray? May I suggest a process that works for me. I don't mean it to be a ritual for anyone, just encouragement.

Find a private place and kneel comfortably and calmly in the center of the room. For a few moments say nothing, just think of him. Just kneel there and feel the closeness of his presence, his warmth, his peace. With humility, express your gratitude for every blessing, every good thing you enjoy. Share with him your problems and fears. Talk to him about each one and pause long enough to receive his counsel. I promise that you will learn his shoulders are broad enough for your burdens.

However, rolling our entire bundle of burdens onto his shoulders is not a simple matter; it requires a majestic leap of faith. Sometimes when we are the loneliest or when we feel the greatest hurt is precisely the time when we feel God is not there, the very time when we feel utterly abandoned by him and by others. But such willingness to trust that he will comfort us, especially in difficult times — such willingness to make that leap of faith toward his embrace when we are least certain of his presence — could well be the most monumental single step of our lives. When we hand our fears and frustrations to him in absolute confidence that he will help us resolve them, when in this way we free our heart and mind and soul of all anxiety, we find in a rather miraculous way that he can instill within us a whole new perspective. He can fill us with "that joy which is unspeakable and full of glory" (Helaman 5:44), even in the midst of our anguish. It is significant to me that this promise of joy that is unspeakable and full of glory came to the brothers Nephi and Lehi, the sons of Helaman, in a terrible moment of trouble. They were in prison, facing oppressive opposition to their work. Yet it was there, amidst such obstacles, that "the Holy Spirit of God did come down from heaven, and did enter into their hearts, and they were filled as if with fire." Then, we read, a voice came to them, "a pleasant voice, that said: Peace, peace be unto you because of your faith." (Helaman 5:45-47.)

I had a childhood experience involving fire and fear and faith. I learned something of God's miraculous gifts and power at the very tender age of nine. Having spent most of my childhood joyfully competing with two older and three younger brothers, I was somewhat of a tomboy at that age. Riding horses, milking cows, shooting marbles, hunting jack rabbits, and, depending on the season, ice skating or swimming in Holt's Pond—these were my favorite ideas for family fun. This all took place, of course, in the humble little hamlet of Enterprise, Utah, an entire community of faith—founded and settled by my great-grandfather.

My heritage was richly steeped in stories of early Mormon courage, so my cousin and I, when we weren't acting like boys, spent most of our time together pretending we were great pioneer women. One day after school we rode our horses to the top of the hill above Andy P. Windsor's farm. There, with great imagination and all the authentic ingredients in hand—one can of beans, two pork chops, two potatoes, two flint stones, a small box of matches (as backup to the flint stones), and a dutch oven—we made preparations for "cooking our grub."

Supper went just fine, and since no pioneer meal could be complete without marshmallows, we set out to find sticks on which to roast them. We were not gone long, but we returned to find a fire completely out of control—at least it appeared out of control to two terrified nine-year-old girls. As it increased in its scope and speed, we could see its direction would take it straight to A. P. Windsor's house, barns, and animals below.

Suddenly we were facing a genuine pioneer problem. True to the faith that our great-grandparents had cherished, we knew that our only hope would have to be heavenly. Instinctively and simultaneously we fell to our knees crying, pleading, and praying vocally for divine help and power. We prayed with our whole hearts, minds, and souls. We prayed as though our very lives depended on it. We certainly prayed as if A. P. Windsor's house depended on it. We prayed as only nine-year-olds know how to pray, with absolute faith, nothing doubting. God was with us on that hilltop that day— and I might say he was with the whole town of Enterprise as well. (I can see the headlines: "Two 9-year-old cooks roast the entire city of Enterprise.") He can and did control our burning bush. I believe it was from that moment on that I came to know, nothing doubting, that God's power is great, and childlike prayers are answered.

I have found, though, as I have weathered more of life's experiences, that it is almost easier to have faith in the miraculous—especially a child's view of the miraculous—than it is to hand over to God our everyday worries, concerns, and anxieties that can accumulate even as a "cloud of darkness." From those same verses about fire given to Nephi and Lehi in prison we read: "What shall we do, that this cloud of darkness may be removed from overshadowing us? And Aminidab said unto them, . . . Ye shall have faith in Christ, . . . and when ye shall do this, the cloud of darkness shall be removed from overshadowing you." (Helaman 5:40-41.)

This brightness of hope and unspeakable joy in God's power and comfort comes, even in everyday matters for me, only as I prayerfully exert my right to his Spirit. If in my heart I go to God the moment I feel even the slightest intimation of fear (or darkness or worry) instead of waiting to let it accumulate, if I speak to God even as my most trusted friend, my wisest counselor, and stay there in my heart or on my knees talking to him long enough, I can always see a ray of light at the edge of those dark shadows. Most often I can then leave his presence with my heart singing. This does not mean that my troubles have dissolved — they probably haven't — but I somehow have the power to see above and around and through those clouds of darkness with greater calm and peacefulness. I know that he will, with time, help me to dissipate them completely.

Out of sorrow and despair we are, through the comforting, protecting grace of God, lifted out of our weakness to the very summit of spiritual, peaceful transcendence that, without the "Father of all comfort" could only be dreamed about from afar.

A French poet, Guillaume Apollinaire, once wrote:

> *Come to the edge.*
> *No, we will fall,*
> *Come to the edge.*
> *No, we will fall.*
> *They came to the edge.*
> *He pushed them, and they flew.*

One of my husband's favorite scriptures is from Isaiah: "Hast thou not heard, that the everlasting God, the Lord, the Creator of the ends of the earth, fainteth not, neither is weary? . . . He giveth power to the faint; and to them that have no might he increaseth strength. . . . They that wait upon the Lord shall renew their strength; they shall mount up with wings as eagles; they shall run, and not be weary; and they shall walk, and not faint." (Isaiah 40:28-31.)

Jeff's ebullient attitude is so incredibly infectious that I don't think many people can be around him very long without feeling they, too, have wings. I have had the opportunity of seeing him put this scripture—and others—into action in his life many, many times. One experience occurred when we were in graduate school. It was a very demanding time for all of us, but especially for Jeff. He was a devoted husband and the loving father of two small children—and was taking a full graduate load in a difficult program at Yale University. To make ends meet on a very limited budget, he taught an institute of religion class at Yale University in New Haven, Connecticut, and one at Amherst College in Massachusetts; the latter required a ninety-mile drive each way every week. He also served as a counselor in the stake presidency. We seemed to have very little money and even less time. And we seemed to be running out of both pretty regularly.

Because of our family situation and the responsibility Jeff felt for us, he determined, with the encouragement of his professors, to take his oral examination considerably ahead of the schedule of his classmates—nearly a year ahead of some of them. He threw himself vigorously into preparation for the exam, but the pressure was immense. He knew his examining committee would be particularly conscious that he was coming to the exam very early and they would be certain not to let him slip past with poor preparation. Worst of all, to fail in an aggressive first try would almost certainly set our schedule back more severely than if we were to wait and go along with the mainstream of students.

For as long as I have known Jeff, the minute he has had a burden of any proportion, he has always begun a fast and taken a discussion of the problem directly to the Lord. I will never forget that night of decision when we had to schedule or not schedule—sort of "To be or not to be," New Haven style. Those were hours of anxiety and unrest and, yes, outright fear—fear of failure, fear of responsibility, fear of overconfidence or lack of confidence, fear of a seemingly limitless number of consequences that would affect at least four people, not just one. It was a heavy burden of responsibility we all felt, but one that was ultimately on Jeff's shoulders.

We were fasting and we were praying. We were living the gospel as well as we knew how. We were trying hard to be whatever it was God wanted us to be, and we were believers. At the close of that day of fasting and as we prayed earnestly over what seemed to us a very serious matter, I think I have never seen any human being so radiant in my whole life. Jeff truly radiated "a brightness of hope" and was filled with "unspeakable joy." Even now, the image of his countenance is still fresh in my mind. His whole being seemed to glow. The only words I remember him speaking at that moment were, "It's going to be okay." And it was. And it is. And it will always be.

That's a pretty ordinary story taken from our own pretty ordinary student days. It is intended to remind us that the Lord "giveth power to the faint; and to them that have no might he increaseth strength." With faith we can "mount up with wings as eagles," into the very arms of "the God of all comfort" who smiles at our childish fears and understands every recurring doubt. He is our Father and he does hear our prayers. And whenever we go to him earnestly seeking his spirit—a privilege unlimited by time or place or circumstance—we will be filled with light and we will be lightened of our load. It is a gift from God.

George MacDonald wrote: "Where the spirit of the Lord is there is liberty; no veil; free sight; clear, radiant insight and perception. Where the Spirit of the Lord is not, there is slavery at all times, dullness, and darkness, and stupidity." (*Getting to Know Jesus* [New York: Ballantine, 1987], p. 5.)

To be honest, I am not interested in any more "dullness, darkness, and stupidity" than I already feel. Why then don't we have the Spirit of the Lord with us more often than we do? Actually, nothing dominated my thoughts when I was younger quite so much as why, when I had so much faith and had at times been able to move a veritable mountain (or at least keep from burning one up!), did I continue to have fears, or to feel "dull, dark, and stupid," as George Mac-Donald would say. That was always a great and very disturbing mystery to me when I was in school, and I thought about it for a long, long time.

As I now look back at it with many more years of experience and perspective, I have wondered if perhaps many of those self-doubts and insecurities come because we actually fear God. Do we still see him as the God of the Old Testament—full of wrath and anger and vengeance? Do we continue to act or perform our duties because we fear his judgment and punishment? Or do we act out of our love for him with the absolute knowledge, nothing doubting, that he truly loves us? He is "the Father of mercies, and the God of all comfort." I now believe that. I want all of us to believe it.

I sheepishly admit there have been too many times in my life when I assumed that God's love for me was conditional, that I somehow had to be absolutely perfect in order to receive it, that some childish thing I had done or thought or said would surely keep me from being worthy of his love. Sometimes I have felt as though my ability to ask for God's deliverance depended totally on my own righteousness. I expect many people have felt that way.

It has been comforting to me to realize that over many years I have been given an unfathomable number of blessings. I have been helped and rewarded beyond my deepest dreams or highest hopes—and all in spite of those imperfections I knew I had and worried about so much. Imperfect, inadequate, unconfident Pat Holland has received all those answers to prayers and all those myriad of blessings. If imperfection can bring such comforts, what must lie ahead of us as we truly do get better at this business of living life perfectly?

Catherine Marshall, whose writings I have come to admire because of her complete trust in God, has written about a moment in her life when she was full of self-dissatisfaction, doubts, questions, and had great fears about her worthiness and continued usefulness to God. She said she urgently asked for his help, and these words of complete comfort came:

"Thou art my beloved child, Catherine. Rest in that love. . . . Stop asking so many questions. Stop all this probing, taking your spiritual temperature. Does the Lord want me to do this? Or that? Is this right? Is that right? This is the source of the confusion you are feeling.

"You are My child, My disciple. I accepted you long ago— *as you are*—as you are growing.

"You are *still* accepted. . . .

"The nervous probing is Satan's doing, to unsettle you, to confuse you, to knock you off the base of your belief. . . .

"*Be not afraid.* [My] joy will sweep away your fear and uncertainties." (*A Closer Walk* [New York: Avon Books, 1987], p. 132.)

With that appeal from someone who wishes to be reassured in order to be useful, may we recall the second half of that scriptural theme from 2 Corinthians: "Who comforteth us in all our tribulation, that we may be able to comfort them which are in any trouble, by the comfort wherewith we ourselves are comforted of God." What a magnificent idea! We are entitled to God's love and reassurance and comfort, at least in part, so we can pass that gift on to others.

The link between God's comfort to us and our comfort, or service, to others is a powerful idea. Such encouragement to magnify God's love through us to other people comes in this marvelous counsel in Dostoyevsky's *The Brothers Karamazov*. Father Zossima is speaking to a woman who fears greatly because of her inadequacies (just like Catherine Marshall and the rest of us), and thus finds herself cut off and distanced from other people.

"Fear nothing and never be afraid," Zossima says, "and don't fret. . . . Can there be a sin which could exceed the love of God? Think only of repentance . . . but dismiss fear altogether. Believe that God loves you as you cannot conceive. . . . It has been said of old that over one repentant sinner there is more joy in heaven than over ten righteous men. Go, and fear not. Be not bitter against men. Be not angry if you are wronged. Forgive. . . .

"If you are penitent, you love," Zossima continues. "And if you love, you are of God. All things are atoned for, all things are saved by love. If I, a sinner, even as you are, am tender with you and have pity on you, how much more will God? Love is such a priceless treasure that you can redeem the whole world by it, and expiate not only your own sins but the sins of others. Go, and be not afraid." (New York: The Modern Library, p. 51.)

That commandment to go, to move outward and upward with confidence in God, is for the express purpose of blessing others, of bringing others to the fullness of faith in God and joy in the gospel of Christ.

One evening I invited my returned missionary son to sit with me and discuss this idea of obtaining confidence in order to bless others. Though it would be hard to believe it now, there was a time in Matt's life when he was quite shy and fearful.

We moved to Provo to assume Jeff's new responsibility at a very difficult time for Matt. He was just beginning the ninth grade, a time of considerable teenage insecurity at best, and surely so in a new community without a single friend. Furthermore, he wore the scarlet letters of "PS" wherever he went—the burdensome label of "president's son."

As he and I sat in our living room talking, he shared with me something he had never told me through those difficult times. He said that as a somewhat frightened and lonely new boy at a new school, he prayed the exact same prayer, virtually word for word, for many, many months. He said, "Every night I would pray and ask: 'Father in heaven, bless me that I can make the varsity basketball team, bless me that I can be a good student, and bless me with enough confidence to make friends.' "

Soon enough all those prayers were answered. He made the varsity team, he was a good student, and he made many, many friends. But, he said to me that night, "It was not until I was serving my mission that I realized I had gone about the confidence matter in entirely the wrong way. It was only in my intense and heartfelt desire to serve others as a missionary that I found what true confidence really was.

"When asking for my own needs in those high school years, I was not reassured. Even now if I ask for his help to have more popularity or to look good in the eyes of others, I lose that confidence. But on my mission when I wanted to reach unbelievers for *their* sake, for what I knew I could give *them*, I had the confidence of Joshua and Jeremiah combined. I knew I could reach them somehow, some way, and I had that terrific self-assurance because it was for someone else's benefit. I will forever see self-confidence in a different way as a result of my mission.

"Confidence," he concluded, "is a gift from God to enable us to serve others."

That same Zossima we referred to earlier in Dostoyevsky's novel reinforces this very important principle, not with a believer like Matt, but with an unbeliever, a woman who has lost her faith and wants to know how to regain it. Not surprisingly he counsels her to serve, to seek out, to comfort others with the very comfort she herself desires to have.

"[You must have] the experience of active love," he tells her. "Strive to love your neighbor actively and indefatigably. Insofar as you advance in love you will grow surer of the reality of God and of the immortality of your soul. If you attain to perfect self-forgetfulness in the love of your neighbor, then you will believe without doubt, and no doubt can enter your soul. This has been tried. This is certain."

God wants so much for us to bless others, to find our lives by losing them, that he frequently and purposefully answers our own prayers, as well as those of others through our acts of caring and comfort. Many times I have heard people say, "I was praying for someone to come, and God sent you. I was lonely, and you walked in the door. I was down until you said hi. I was blue and you wrote me that note. I was fearful until you took my hand." These are the experiences of active love.

The following story was shared with me by one of our BYU students, David Rodebeck. We can learn much from the actions of two young women who understand that God's comfort and compassion will often need to come to others through us.

These two students are the sort of Christians we all would like to be. They even study the holy scriptures every day, for the express purpose of learning more of the attributes and doctrines of Jesus Christ. And, quietly but inevitably, those divine attributes rub off. The two students, of course, have their share of difficulties, some of which are not small, but not so serious, perhaps, as the struggles of someone else.

As they walked around the Provo Temple one evening, they saw a young Indian girl, a freshman at BYU, who was sitting outside the gates of the temple, bathing the grass with her tears. She was an excellent student, and all her life she had dreamed of attending BYU. Finally, her dream had come true. But now, mere weeks later, she had received terrible grades on her midterms, and, far away, her family was falling apart, with her mother in danger for her life at the hands of her drunken father. The girl's money was gone, employment was nowhere to be found, she had no friends, and she was losing her health and her grades because of it all. No wonder she wept! No wonder she had gone to the temple grounds to pray!

These two young people, bearing in their countenances the image of comforting angels, stopped to talk. They talked for more than an hour; then the three went their separate ways. But their ways did not separate. Every few days, whether they had time or not, the two would visit this fearful girl or leave a note on her door. Each time the message was essentially the same, though not in precisely these words: "We love you. God loves you. Let your heart be comforted, 'for all flesh is in mine hands.' 'God is our refuge and strength, a very present help in trouble. . . . Be still, and know that I am God.' " (D&C 101:16; Psalm 46:1, 10.)

Of course, the trials did not disappear quickly; some of them did not even improve. But this girl changed. I do not know what she knew of God before that lonely night in October—obviously, she knew enough to pray—but she knows something about him now that she did not know before. In the form of two young women just her age, she has seen "the God of all comfort." She knows that again and again he sent those two disciples to her rescue, two young women whose last names she does not even know. And she knows he sent them because he loves her.

Our Father in heaven loves us all, in spite of our fears and mistakes and perceived lack of talents and confidence. As we fully embrace this truth, it will fill us with a brightness of hope and unspeakable joy.

Chapter 6

A WOMAN'S PERSPECTIVE ON THE PRIESTHOOD

It seems clear that our greatest task is to live worthily enough to know step by step what the Lord's will is regarding us, remembering that occasionally what we may want to do today because of the trends and vanities of the world may not be what we covenanted to do long ago. Finally we must, like Mary, say, "Be it unto me according to thy word."

President Spencer W. Kimball stated in a fireside address to the women of the Church, "We had full equality as his spirit children." He then went on to say that "within those great assurances, however, our roles and assignments differ." *(Ensign, November 1979, p. 102.)*

I believe that every one of us has a specific mission to fulfill on this earth. "There is a time appointed for every man [and woman], according as [their] works shall be." (D&C 121:25.) "For all have not every gift given unto them; for there are many gifts, and to every man [and woman] is given a gift by the Spirit of God. To some is given one, and to some is given another, that all may be profited thereby." (D&C 46:11-12.)

I believe that we made sacred promises in premortal councils regarding our role in building the kingdom of God on earth. In turn we were promised the gifts and powers necessary to fulfill those very special tasks. I would like to quote from President Kimball again: "Remember, in the world be-

49

fore we came here, faithful women were given certain assignments while faithful men were foreordained to certain priesthood tasks. . . . You are accountable for those things which long ago were expected of you just as are those we sustain as prophets and apostles!" (*Ensign*, November 1979, p. 102.) I also believe that those assignments and roles differ as much from woman to woman as they do from man to woman.

We've all been taught to have role models. It is good to have someone to look up to. However, there is great danger in wanting to be too much like someone else. We will feel competitive jealousy and self-defeat. No two people are the same. Some women have been given large families, some small, and some none at all. Many wives are exercising their gifts and talents in sustaining their husbands in their work as community leaders, business leaders, stake presidents, bishops, or General Authorities, and encouraging their children's development. Other women apply their gifts and talents directly as leaders in their own right. Still other women combine both the supportive and the direct roles in exercising their gifts and thus serve in dual capacities. For example, we all know there was a great difference between the assignments of Mary Fielding Smith and Eliza R. Snow, yet both eagerly sought the will of the Lord. Both sought marriage and family. Both gave everything they had to the kingdom.

It seems clear, then, that our greatest task is to live worthily enough to know step by step what the Lord's will is regarding us, remembering that occasionally what we may want to do today because of the trends and vanities of the world may not be what we covenanted to do long ago. We should be willing to live and pray like Mary, the mother of Jesus, when she said to the angel who had just given her the assignment, "Be it unto me according to thy word." (Luke 1:38.)

Let me use a personal example for a moment. Sister Ardeth Kapp, one of my dearest friends, is one of the purest, sweetest, strongest women I know. Her husband, Heber, is a great strength and served as our stake president in Bountiful, Utah. The Kapps have not yet been blessed with any children. Joan Quinn is another dear friend and also one of the purest, sweetest, strongest women I know. Her husband, Ed, is a brilliant and able man — another stable and inspiring influence in our lives. The Quinns have been blessed with twelve children. My husband and I are doing what we can in the kingdom. We have been blessed with three children.

Some women I know have not yet been blessed with a mate or marriage. Yet they too are building the kingdom every day and blessing me personally through our association. Six very different examples are Maren Mouritsen and Marilyn Arnold, whom I treasure as dear friends at BYU; Carolyn Rasmus, with whom I worked in the Young Women; and three who have served as my husband's gifted secretaries, Randi Greene, Janet Calder, and Jan Nelson, whose contribution to our lives is personal as well as professional. Obviously the list of women who bless me and bless the Church could go on and on. My point is that Ardeth, Joan, Carolyn, Maren, Marilyn, Randi, Janet, and Jan are all very different. Presently, we all have different roles in life. Perhaps these roles will change for each of us in the years ahead. Yet we love each other very much and we have always loved the men in our lives — fathers, brothers, friends, husbands, sons. And we love the priesthood. Each of us must want the right things, must pursue the right things, and must give all that we have to the kingdom with an eye single to God and the covenants we've made. As President David O. McKay often quoted, "Whate'er thou art, act well thy part."

Of course, to do this we must live close to the Spirit through prayer, study, and righteous living in order to avoid the distractions and more selfish goals that might frustrate the Lord's design for us and cause us to forsake it. For when that occurs, I believe, we will feel frustrated and forsaken and not feel the peace and security that can come only from ful-

51

filling the mission that is ours. To paraphrase John F. Kennedy, ask not what the kingdom can do for you, but what you can do for the kingdom. Whatever our role is, we must seek it through righteous living and personal revelation. We must not lean on the arm of flesh nor the philosophies of men—or women. We must have our own personal liahona. That is exactly what the Lord expects of priesthood bearers also.

In fact, all of this is to stress that we cherish differences—not only from man to woman but from woman to woman. In discussing the relationship of women with their special assignments and men with their priesthood tasks, I find it much more useful to speak in the language of obligations and responsibilities, rather than in the language of "rights." Frankly, I'm weary of rights fights, rights movements, and rights marches—male, female, or any other kind. So I want to speak of obligations, and I cite as a source these impressive words of Aleksandr Solzhenitsyn: "It is time, in the West, to defend not so much human *rights* as human *obligations*. Destructive and irresponsible freedom has been granted boundless space [in the free world]. [Western] Society appears to have little defense against . . . human decadence, . . . [and] the misuse of liberty for moral violence. . . . This is considered to be part of freedom, . . . [but] life organized [so] legalistically has thus shown its inability to defend itself against the corrosion of evil." ("A World Split Apart," *National Review,* July 7, 1978, p. 838. Italics added.)

I believe that if we respond to our responsibilities, our rights will take care of themselves—for male or female. As I was supporting my husband through his Ph.D. at Yale University, our neighbor who was doing his residency in psychiatry commented one day that I was showing overt signs of weariness. Out of concern and intended helpfulness, this neighbor said, "Pat, why don't you stand up for your rights and say to heck with all of this?" At that time I knew through prayer that my rights, whatever they were, had to be put in the perspective of my obligation to pursue long-range goals. I certainly never thought Jeff's degree was only for *his* future. And he never thought the children belonged only to *me*. We were in all of this together, and we didn't waste any energy shouting about rights. That time was intense and difficult, but it lasted only three years. As a direct consequence of my supportive role then, I now have time, means, and wonderful opportunities to pursue many of my interests and talents in addition to being very much a wife and mother. Furthermore, I know — and love knowing — that my ultimate role and mission will always include the particular joys of providing loving and wise support to others as they fulfill their own assignments.

If our role or assignment is a supportive one — and many of us will often have that role — we must study and prepare ourselves enough to articulate to the world that we are not apologizing for strengthening the home; rather, we are pursuing our highest priorities, personally, socially, and theologically.

Several years ago I attended with my husband a two-week seminar in Israel for Moslems, Christians, and Jews. The participants were editors of newspapers, former ambassadors, priests, rabbis, university presidents, and professors. During that two-week period, nearly every participant made it a point to ask me about Mormon women. Though many other wives attending the seminar were living as I do — staying at home, raising children — I was the one singled out. As Mormon women, we *do* stand out. We should be a light on a hill. It is our responsibility to study, prepare, and work at being articulate enough to teach the truth about our priorities and privileges as women in the Church.

In light of such obligations (as opposed to rights), consider the revelation we have all come to love so much from Joseph Smith's experience in the Liberty jail. Isn't it ironic that the scene of so few rights, of so little freedom, and of so much abusive authority should be the setting for such profound revelation on rights and freedom and the use of authority? I suppose that in just such settings the Lord really has our full attention and uses our pain (in this case, Joseph Smith's pain) as a megaphone for very significant instructions. These familiar passages are lengthy but beautiful and very important:

"Behold, there are many called, but few are chosen. And why are they not chosen? Because their hearts are set so much upon the things of this world, and aspire to the honors of men, that they do not learn this one lesson—that the rights of the priesthood are inseparably connected with the powers of heaven, and that the powers of heaven cannot be controlled nor handled only upon the principles of righteousness.

"That they may be conferred upon us, it is true; but when we undertake to cover our sins, or to gratify our pride, our vain ambition, or to exercise control or dominion or compulsion upon the souls of the children of men, in any degree of unrighteousness, behold, the heavens withdraw themselves; the Spirit of the Lord is grieved; and when it is withdrawn, Amen to the priesthood or the authority of that man. . . .

"We have learned by sad experience that it is the nature and disposition of almost all men, as soon as they get a little authority, as they suppose, they will immediately begin to exercise unrighteous dominion. . . .

"No power or influence can or ought to be maintained by virtue of the priesthood, only by persuasion, by long-suffering, by gentleness and meekness, and by love unfeigned; by kindness, and pure knowledge, which shall greatly enlarge the soul without hypocrisy, and without guile—reproving betimes with sharpness, when moved upon by the Holy Ghost; and then showing forth afterwards an increase of love toward him whom thou hast reproved, lest he esteem thee to be his enemy; that he may know that thy faithfulness is stronger than the cords of death.

"Let thy bowels also be full of charity towards all men, and to the household of faith, and let virtue garnish thy thoughts unceasingly; then shall thy confidence wax strong in the presence of God; and the doctrine of the priesthood shall distil upon thy soul as the dews from heaven. The Holy Ghost shall be thy constant companion, and thy scepter an unchanging scepter of righteousness and truth; and thy dominion shall be an everlasting dominion, and without compulsory means it shall flow unto thee forever and ever." (D&C 121:34-37, 39, 41-46.)

It seems important to note that as the Lord speaks to the Prophet Joseph of rights—and he does speak of rights—they are conveyed by and supported by and surrounded with all kinds of instructions about obligations and responsibilities. The privileges of the priesthood are not isolated from duties and neither are the privileges of women. Note the opening lines—Why are so few chosen after so many have been called? "Because their hearts are set so much upon the things of this world, and aspire to the honors of men." (D&C 121:35.)

This world is *not* our ultimate home; and while we do have to live here, and live here constructively, we are not ever, as Christians, really of this world. And we do not seek its praise. President Kimball said: "Among the real heroines in the world who will come into the Church are women who are more concerned with being righteous than with being selfish. These real heroines have true humility, which places a higher value on integrity than on visibility. Remember, it is as wrong to do things just to be seen of women as it is to do things to be seen of men." (*Ensign,* November 1979, p. 104.)

I cannot speak for anyone but myself, but for me there is not now nor will there ever be a political issue of *this* world more important to me than my eternal life in the *next*. It isn't that I believe earthly political issues are not important. They are. It is just that the eternal kingdom of God is *all* important. If I want to be chosen as well as called (incidentally, a privilege, not a right, which I desire very much), then my devotion must be to a ruler who is King of kings and Lord of lords, who knows me and knows my needs, and to whom I must be loyal.

I take this digression simply to make the point again that this world, work in it as we must, is not our home. Our hearts must not be set too much upon things here. We must not seek the praise of humans more than the praise of God. That is, we must not if we believe the kingdom of God, as we now know it in the institutional Church of Jesus Christ of Latter-day Saints, is rolling forward under God's hand so that the kingdom of heaven may come. Nothing must divert us from that belief and that mission, to fully realize the triumphant return of the Prince of Peace. I promise you that this return will be orchestrated through the Church with its eternal mission, and not through politics with its temporal demise. In that sense, members of the Church are all foot soldiers in the same army, a battalion led by Christ and drilled by the prophets. (That is a righteous infantry, for which women will volunteer and won't have to be drafted.)

Returning to section 121, why have people trapped in this worldly concern not remembered just this one lesson: "That the rights of the priesthood [and womanhood] are inseparably connected with the powers of heaven and that the powers of heaven cannot be controlled nor handled only [or except] upon the principles of righteousness"? (D&C 121:36.)

Isn't it interesting that rights, as approached in this language from the Lord, seem to say nothing male or female. Though the verse speaks of priesthood, surely every woman's rights and powers are conditional on *exactly* the same premise. Those are the rules of the game for everyone—male, female, black, white, bond, or free. (See 2 Nephi 26:33.) Can it be that if we keep the commandments—commandments that are common to us all—then the day will come when, in eternal recompense, God will say to everyone, male and female, "Well done, thou good and faithful servant: thou hast been faithful over a few things, I will make thee ruler over many things"? (Matthew 25:21.)

In section 121, we note the resolution of many potential problems. For example, verse 37 says we are not "to cover our sins, or to gratify our pride, [or] our vain ambition." Are those commandments only for males? Only for females? Or for both? We are also told in that verse not "to exercise control or dominion or compulsion" on others in unrighteousness. Is that counsel only for men? Only for women? Or for both? How should men exercise influence in the kingdom of God? How should women? Words like *persuasion, long-suffering, gentleness, meekness, love unfeigned* — are those male qualities? Or female qualities? Or are they finally just some nonnegotiable qualities of a Christlike life, male and female? I think the latter.

And referring to the last two verses of section 121, are women the only ones who should have their bowels "full of charity"? Are men the only ones who should "garnish" their thoughts with virtue? Is the Holy Ghost a "constant companion" only for priesthood bearers? Are women the only ones who might hold "an unchanging scepter of righteousness and truth"? Will either a man or a woman have "an everlasting dominion" without the other? The questions give their own answers in the asking. When the Lord speaks of righteousness, there isn't any conflict over gender.

All of this leads me to ask, Why is such incredible energy expended by Latter-day Saint men and/or women over issues like women and the priesthood?

I offer this answer to my own question: It seems to me that if there is a conflict, it is because someone, male or female, isn't living the gospel of Jesus Christ. Now, I did not say that the person who has the concern isn't living the gospel. That may or may not be true. What I said is that *someone* isn't living the gospel. A woman in pain may be living the gospel the very best she knows how and yet still find herself hurting. But if that is the case, I still believe that *someone* in her life isn't living — or hasn't lived — the gospel. Somewhere, somehow, promises have not been kept or obligations have not been honored, and thus the hurt. But that is not a priesthood problem. The most we can say is that it is a person problem. Thus, the responsibility is on us all, male and female, to live as section 121 prescribes and as every other Christlike example requires. With that kind of loving male and female relationship and with those kinds of promises, the pain and despair and frustrations of this world disappear. I believe that with all my heart. The answers to our challenges are gospel answers (priesthood answers, if you will), not male or female answers. They are promises to the faithful.

A final concrete example comes from one not of our faith. Elder Dallin H. Oaks told me of this inspiring application of the point I am trying to make about choices and obligations. As a young law professor, Elder Oaks was closely associated with Supreme Court Justice Lewis M. Powell. Justice Powell's daughter was herself a recent graduate of a fine law school, following which she began a successful law practice and a marriage almost simultaneously. Some time thereafter she had her first child. In paying a courtesy call as a family friend, Elder Oaks was pleasantly surprised to find this young mother at home with her child full time. When he asked about this decision, she replied, "Oh, I may go back to the law sometime, but not now. For me the issue was simple. Anyone could take care of my clients, but only I can be the mother of this child." What an incisive answer to an issue she says was simple! And it does seem to have been simple because she approached it not in terms of rights, but first and foremost in terms of responsibilities. I think the issue would not have been so simple if her attitude had been, "It's my body," or "It's my career," or "It's my life." But her concern was for her obligations. When framed that way, the issue and the answer were simple.

We all have rights and the freedom to pursue them. That much the Lord has promised us. I believe, then, that the crucial point we need to come to as Latter-day Saint men and women is not to allow ourselves to feel forced into righteous choices, but to come to them of our own free and anxious will. In feeling compelled or forced lies some of the pain and frustration and depression we hear about. We should seek diligently and prayerfully the light that would quicken our hearts and minds to truly desire the outcomes we make in righteous decisions. Our prayers ought to be to see as God sees, to flip the switch in our minds so we may see things eternally. If we listen too often to the voices of the world, we will become confused and tainted. We must anchor ourselves in the Spirit, and that requires daily vigilance.

In Galatians 5 from the New English Translation we find this conclusion:

"You, my friends, were called to be free men [in other words, you have your rights]; only do not turn your freedom [your rights] into license for your lower nature. . . . If you go on fighting one another, tooth and nail, all you can expect is mutual destruction. . . .

"The harvest of the Spirit is love, joy, peace, patience, kindness, goodness, fidelity, gentleness, and self-control. We must not be conceited, challenging one another to rivalry, jealous of one another. If the Spirit is the source of our life, let the Spirit also direct our course." (Galatians 5:13, 22, 25-26.)

Chapter 7

THE MANY
FACES OF EVE

*We live in an enormously stressful world. Everyone
seems to be hurried or worried or both. There is increasing
concern about what is expected of us, how much we
should expect from ourselves, and how we can find the
time, energy, and means to accomplish it all. If we are
to succeed, we must stay centered and settled. We must
make order out of chaos.*

Before we, as daughters of Eve, ever blossom to the
full fruition of our femaleness, we each wear a variety
of faces in the different roles we play in the drama of
life – daughters, mothers, sisters, wives, neighbors, and
friends, to name just a few. Our countenances display charity,
envy, patience, anxiety, pride, humility, generosity, greed,
peace, perplexity. These portraits mirror joy and grief together, and through this exchange the lines are "woven fine."
We are all learning of God's slow, steady way of sculpturing
the experiences that cannot be escaped "till we have *our* face."

Which face is really mine? What is my role in life? What
if the faces change so fast and the demands become so great
that we hardly know who we are *any* of the time? How can
we ever hope to be in control *all* of the time?

May I try to give some modest reassurances. First and
most important, if we look closely in those many-mirrored
faces, we will always see God's infinite care in the process of
making us who we are and what we are becoming. We see

the gentle way he kneels to brush back our hair or even to wipe away a tear. He adjusts the angle of the light and works his wonders with lines and scars and shadows. Ever so softly he whispers for us to endure difficulty or discouragement for what it may hold of illumination and eternal beauty. Under his hand our inner person becomes the outer person, and the artist shapes his perfect image.

While we participate in this process and reflect in sanctity and solitude, these perceptions and impressions of our relationship to our Father in heaven can give us great peace and purpose. When we embrace these healing moments of worship, it is easier for us to keep this perspective and not succumb to the constant swirl of faces and roles and activities. With the complexities of rapid change in today's world, it is easy to lose sight of our divine possibility or even to value our viability. In the rigorous demand of it all, we may wonder whether we can simply survive, let alone triumph.

In his book *In Search of the Simple Life,* David E. Shi has written: "Americans today lead lives of 'quiet desperation.' Under all the glamour and glitter of affluence is the disturbing fact that the three most frequently prescribed drugs [in America] are an ulcer medication, a hypertension reliever and a tranquilizer." (Layton, Utah: Gibbs M. Smith, 1986, p. 1.)

We live in an enormously stressful world. Everyone seems to be either hurried or worried or both. There are pressures of pacing ourselves with many time demands, and there seem to be increasing worries about what is expected of us, how much we should expect from ourselves, and how we can find the time, energy, and means to accomplish it all.

The scourge of our times is anxiety. Perhaps some of our anxiety comes, ironically, because the bounty and the blessings of our times have provided us with opportunities and choices our ancestors could never have considered. With automation and technology we have more discretionary time. With greater knowledge we are enjoying better health and more energy. And with more affluence we now have more opportunities to provide growth and special experiences for ourselves and our families. Our mothers and their mothers before them could not have dreamed of such freedom to choose, nor the abundance of such choices.

These blessings, however, add immensely to our anxiety when the choices we face suggest contention not only between right and wrong but, more often, between right and right. Should I car pool the kids to one more ballet lesson or take a class on "How to be a better mother"? Do I spend the evening with my husband or do I run off to the chapel to hear the lecture on "What every man wants from his wife"? We worry and wonder if we should study to obtain more rewarding relationships or spend the needed time to cultivate them. And who comes first: our husband? our children? the Church? our extended family? our neighbors? nonmembers? the dead? And what about ourselves?

Sometimes we know not where we should turn, nor which task should be done first. We feel frustrated, sometimes frightened, and often utterly fatigued. And too often we may feel like absolute failures. Where do we go for help? How do we stay fixed and focused? How do we stay centered and settled instead of floundering in a mindless mass of confusion? In short, how do we make order out of chaos?

I choose to believe that the Lord would not place us in this lone and dreary world without a blueprint for living. In Doctrine and Covenants 52:14 we read: "And again, I will give unto you a pattern in all things, that ye may not be deceived." He has given us patterns in the scriptures, and he has given us patterns in the temple ceremony.

I have chosen the patterns of the temple to share my own personal unveiling of the faces I have been asked to wear. I humbly pray that through my own intimate sharing, you may find a few threads of applicability as you search for your individual identity and eternal certainty.

The temple is highly symbolic. It has been called the University of the Lord. I find myself continually learning when

I attend the temple with an expansive mind. I strive to exercise, to stretch, to look for deeper meaning. I look for parallels and symbols. I look for themes and motifs just as I would in a Bach or a Mozart composition, and I look for patterns — repeated patterns.

My habit of looking for sacred symbols and my testimony of finding answers to personal problems were passed on from mother to daughter to granddaughter to me. I have learned through generations of Eve's daughters the very close connection between our temporal challenges and the spiritual world, and how one assists the other as it pertains to those who attend the temple. So that you will understand my deep feelings about this, I have chosen to share my first experience about the temple's sustaining power.

I was twelve years old, living in Enterprise, Utah, when my parents were called to be temple workers in the St. George Temple, fifty miles away. In telling me of their call, my mother spoke to me of what temples were, why people serve there, and what spiritual experiences some of the saints have had there. Certainly she believed that the seen and unseen worlds meet and mingle in the temple. My duties were to get excused early from school once a week and hurry home to tend five unruly brothers, the youngest of whom was just a toddler. I remember complaining about this assignment one day, and I will never forget the power with which my mother said, "When Daddy and I were set apart for this assignment, we were promised that our family would be blessed and protected, even by 'attending angels.' "

Late one afternoon on one of my parents' temple days, when I was feeling particularly exhausted from providing entertainment for my young charges, I put the baby in a buggy and, with the other boys, walked five blocks to visit with my grandmother.

After a warm greeting, Grandma suggested that we play on the lawn while she went to the store for refreshments. I was distracted with the other children and didn't notice the baby beginning to toddle after his grandmother. Suddenly, and with great fear, I realized that he was out of sight. Instinctively I ran toward the car just in time to see the back wheel turn completely over his small head, crushing it into the gravel beneath. In panic I screamed at the top of my lungs. My grandmother felt the distinct bump, heard my scream, and knew exactly what had happened. However, instead of stopping the car, she panicked and drove back over him again. Twice the wheel of the car moved completely over the head of this beloved baby brother for whom I had been given full responsibility.

The wailing of two hysterical voices quickly caught the attention of my grandfather. He dashed from the house and gathered up the baby (who my grandmother and I were sure was dead), and the three of them frantically drove fifty miles to the nearest doctor. I prayed and cried—cried and prayed. However, children remember promises made even when adults might forget, and I was curiously calm and comforted. I remembered the part about "attending angels."

After what seemed like an eternity, my grandparents called and reported that the baby was fine. He had a badly scratched face where the tire had scraped his head and cheek, but there was no cranial damage. Yet twice I had clearly seen the force of that wheel on his head.

At age twelve one cannot know many spiritual things. I especially did not know what went on in the temple of God. But I knew from *my* experience that it was sacred, and that hovering near, with approval and protection, were heavenly angels. I knew something of heavenly help beyond the veil.

In Doctrine and Covenants 109, that section which teaches us of the holiness of the temple, verse 22 reads: "We ask thee, Holy Father, that thy servants may go forth from this house armed with thy power, and that thy name may be upon them, and thy glory be round about them, and thine angels have charge over them."

That is a powerful promise to those who feel overwhelmed

with the pressures and stresses of daily living, a power and promise I first encountered at twelve years of age. Now, with the many experiences I have had since that age, I can declare that this is true. The temple provides protection and it provides patterns and promises that can settle and strengthen and stabilize us, however anxious our times. If we master the principles taught there, we will receive the promise the Lord gave us through Isaiah: "I will fasten him [or her] as a nail in a sure place." (Isaiah 23:23.)

The Lord often allows us to wallow in mindless confusion before the teacher within us follows the path that lightens our way. Jeff and I were young married graduate students with two babies and heavy church assignments when President Harold B. Lee shared a prophet's counsel on "order in chaos." An anxious physician, worried that, because of his profession and church responsibilities, he was neglecting his own son, asked President Lee, "How should I handle my time? What is most important in life? How do I do it all?" President Lee replied, "A man's first responsibility is to himself, then to his family, then to the Church, realizing that we have responsibilities to excel in our professions as well." He then stressed that a man must first take care of his own health, both physically and emotionally, before he can be a blessing to others.

As a young woman I wrestled with this counsel, considering carefully how one taking care of herself first manages to lose herself for others. As the years passed, I saw how the truth in President Lee's counsel seemed to fit perfectly the order spoken of in the temple. The temple teaches priorities, it teaches order, it teaches growth, it teaches joy and fulfillment. Consider the following teachings from the temple (I have taken the words from the scriptures so that I will not inappropriately trifle with sacred things).

In the fourth chapter of Abraham, the Gods plan the creation of the earth and all life thereon. In these plans (which take thirty-one verses to outline), the word or a form of the word *order* is used sixteen times. The Gods organize and give order to every living thing. "And the Gods said: We will do everything that we have said, and organize them; and they will become very obedient." (Abraham 4:31.) If we are to become like the Gods, we will begin with order. We will choose to obey the laws and principles of heaven which lead to order.

One of the first truths taught in the temple is that "every living thing shall fill the measure of its creation." That is a powerful commandment! Consider it in light of President Lee's counsel. I must admit that when I first heard this directive I thought it meant only procreation: having issue, bearing offspring. I am sure that is the most important part of its meaning, but much of the temple ceremony is symbolic, so surely there are multiple meanings in that statement as well. How else does a woman fill the measure of her creation? How does she become all that her heavenly parents intend her to be? Growth, fulfillment, reaching, stretching, and developing our talents are part of the process of becoming like God, the ultimate "measure of our creation."

How can we be fully successful wives or mothers or missionaries or temple workers or citizens or neighbors if we are not trying to bring our best self to these tasks? Surely that is why President Lee said we need to be strong physically and emotionally in order to help others be strong. That is the order of creation.

Anyone who reads a newspaper or magazine is constantly reminded that proper diet, appropriate exercise, and plenty of rest increase our daily capacities as well as our life span. But all too many of us put off even these minimal efforts, thinking our family, our neighbors, and our other many responsibilities come first. Yet in doing so, we put at risk the thing these people need most from us: our healthiest, happiest, heartiest self. When they ask for bread, let us not be so weary and unhealthy that we give them a stone.

The issue for me, then, is accepting that we are worth the time and effort it takes to achieve the full measure of our creation, and believing that it is not selfish, wrong, or evil. It is, in fact, essential to our spiritual development.

My oldest child tried to teach me this principle years ago. I had not been feeling well on a day I had promised to take this then three-year-old son to the zoo. As my aches and pains increased, I finally said in exasperation, "Matthew, I don't know if we should go to the zoo and take care of you or if we should stay home and take care of mother." He looked up at me for a moment with his big brown eyes and then stated emphatically, "Mama, I think *you* should take care of *you*, so *you* can take care of *me*." He was wise enough even at that age to know where his best interests were ultimately served. Unless we take care of ourselves, it's virtually impossible to properly take care of others.

Medical experts are confirming, from studying people who are overworried as well as overworked, that many illnesses are stress related. Therefore, the basic questions to ask while selflessly serving others are, How much tension in our lives is too much? When does it become counterproductive? Jennifer James, formerly of the psychiatry department at the University of Washington, gives us some suggestions:

"Everyone needs a certain amount of body tension. It keeps us upright. But how much is too much? Have you checked your body lately? How are you feeling? How about your neck—how stiff is it? Or your shoulders? Can you find your balance? Are you centered? Are you irritable? Have you yelled at anyone lately? How about your stomach? Your stomach will always tell you the truth, unless you give it antacid and teach it to lie. We know how to tell that we're tense, but we sometimes ignore it. The question is, why?

"We know that exercise gives almost instant relief from tension. We know that if we give up caffeine and sugar, stop smoking, and give up being workaholics we can relieve stress. But we don't choose to.

"Some people think that someone else will take the responsibility—their parents, their friends, their spouse, maybe even Mother Nature. But if you don't take care of yourself, no one else will. What is your choice? Why are you choosing not to take care of your stresses? Do you think that you don't deserve to feel better? You do." (*Success Is the Quality of Your Journey* [New York: Newmarket Press, 1986], p. 23.)

Our physician in Provo, who is also one of my stake leaders, scolded me one day during an examination when he noted that the lowest thing on my list of concerns was caring for myself. He looked me sternly in the eye and asked me to remember the promises made in the endowment, and then he asked me to think about the promises of the initiatory ordinances. Our children and our children's children and all of our posterity depend in some measure upon our physical health. Caring for our physical health is, then, a prerequisite to President Lee's second priority—emotional health.

We have been created to become like the Gods. That means we already have inherent within us godly attributes, the greatest of which is Christlike charity. And the key to emotional health is charity—love. Joy comes from loving and being loved. When this divine attribute is at work in our feelings for our family, our neighbors, our God, *and ourselves,* we feel joy. When it is immobilized with conflict toward others, toward God, or toward ourselves, we are depressed in our growth and we become depressed in our attitude.

Depression, conflict, or negativism is often a message to us that we are not growing toward the full measure for which God has created us. Our pain—emotional pain—is a demand that we stop and take time for change in our life because we may be getting off course. As Elder Richard L. Evans used to say, "What's the use of running if you are on the wrong road?" Of course, we all get on the wrong road occasionally; we all have conflicts and discouragement and make mistakes sometimes. But I love this thought from Sister Teres Lizia: "If you are willing to serenely bear the trial of [personal disappointment and weakness] then you will be for Jesus a pleasant place of shelter." The key word is *serene.* If we bear our weaknesses and mistakes, hurt feelings and misgivings, *serenely,* and if we accept the down times and learn from them, they will pass and return less often.

We receive mixed messages today that self-love and a sense of self-worth are forms of selfishness and conceit. However, I know from my own experience that when I don't fully accept myself and all of my warts, blemishes, and imperfections, I am crippled in my charity toward God and my neighbors. Let me encourage you not to feel guilty as you aspire to appropriate self-love, which comes in part by honest self-knowledge and acceptance.

Perhaps we all agree on this premise, yet we are unsure about the process for achieving it. It is easier for me to understand when I see it applied to someone other than myself. For example, I begin to love my neighbor when I create experiences that will allow me to get to know her and understand why she acts and reacts the way she does in different circumstances and settings. The more I know her, the more I understand her. And the more I understand her, the more I love her. My knowledge of God also increases when I spend more time with him in prayer, in his holy writ, and in his service. And the more I know and understand him, the more I love him.

This same principle applies to ourselves. Appropriately loving ourselves requires looking within ourselves deeply, honestly, and, as Sister Teres suggests, serenely. It requires a loving look at the bad as well as the good. The more we understand and know, the more we love.

Our Father in heaven needs us as we are, as we are growing to become. He has intentionally made us different from one another so that even with our imperfections we can fulfill his purposes. My greatest misery comes when I feel I have to fit what others are doing, or what I think others expect of me. I am most happy when I am comfortable being me and trying to do what my Father in heaven and I expect me to be.

For many years I tried to measure the ofttimes quiet,

reflective, thoughtful Pat Holland against the robust, bubbly, talkative, and energetic Jeff Holland and others with like qualities. I have learned through several fatiguing failures that you can't have joy in being bubbly if you are not a bubbly person. It is a contradiction in terms. I have given up seeing myself as a flawed person because my energy level is lower than Jeff's, and I don't talk as much as he does, nor as fast. Giving this up has freed me to embrace and rejoice in my own manner and personality in the measure of *my* creation. Ironically, that has allowed me to admire and enjoy Jeff's ebullience even more.

Somewhere, somehow the Lord "blipped the message onto my screen" that my personality was created to fit precisely the mission and talents he gave me. For example, the quieter, calmer talent of playing the piano reveals much about the real Pat Holland. I would never have learned to play the piano if I hadn't enjoyed the long hours of solitude required for its development. This same principle applies to my love of writing, reading, meditation, and especially teaching and talking with my children. Miraculously, I have found that I have untold abundant sources of energy to be myself. But the moment I indulge in imitation of my neighbor, I feel fractured and fatigued and find myself forever swimming upstream. When we frustrate God's plan for us, we deprive this world and God's kingdom of our unique contributions, and a serious schism settles in our soul. God never gave us any task beyond our ability to accomplish it. We just have to be willing to do it our own way. We will always have enough resources for being who we are and what we can become.

Self-knowledge is not selfish; it is a priority spiritual journey. Paul exhorts, "Examine yourselves, whether ye be in the faith; prove your own selves. Know ye not your own selves, how that Jesus Christ is in you?" (2 Corinthians 13:5.) We must each prepare right now to intensify our own inner journey. In no other structure—in no other setting—can we receive more illuminating light shining on our self-realization

70

than in the temple. As we go there often, the Lord will teach us that we have been created that we might have joy, and joy comes as we embrace the true measure of our creation.

In the Doctrine and Covenants we read: "Do thou grant, Holy Father, that all those who shall worship in this house may be taught words of wisdom . . . and that they may grow up in thee, and receive a fulness of the Holy Ghost, and be organized according to thy laws, and be prepared to obtain every needful thing." (D&C 109:14-15.)

After our physical and emotional health, our next priority is family, and a Latter-day Saint family begins where it ends: with a man and a woman, united in the temple of the Lord. In the temple we come to understand that "neither is the man without the woman, neither the woman without the man, in the Lord." (1 Corinthians 11:11.) Abraham 4:27 reads: "So the Gods went down to organize man in their own image, in the image of the Gods to form they him, male and female to form they them." It takes both male and female to make the complete image of God.

When we were married, Jeff and I became a new entity. Together, Jeff, with all of his maleness, and I, with all of my femaleness, create a complete and unfragmented new whole. When we are integrated, Jeff shares in my femininity and I share in his masculinity so that the whole, fitly joined together, is much greater than the sum of the parts. But Satan does not want us to be one. He knows that the marital body in its unity and wholeness has great power, and he insidiously insists upon independence, individuation, and autonomy. So eventually the body is fragmented—broken.

May I share a thought from Madeleine L'Engle: "The original relationship between male and female was meant to be one of mutual fulfillment and joy, but that relationship was broken, to our grief, and turned into one of suspicion and warfare, misunderstanding and exclusion, and will not be fully restored until the end of time. Nevertheless, we are given enough glimpses of the original relationship so that we should

71

be able to rejoice in our participation." *(The Irrational Season* [New York: The Seabury Press, 1977], p. 9.)

There are two perspectives that I keep in mind because they help maintain oneness for Pat and Jeff Holland.

First, we come together as equal, whole, developing, and contributing partners. Most of our movement together is in a lateral relationship. We move side by side, together, simultaneously, much like doubly-yoked oxen. But there are times when, for the sake of godly progress and development, I follow my husband in a vertical relationship. A house of God is a house of order. We all fall in line behind someone in that straight course that leads to eternal bliss. I am so grateful that I fall in line with Jeff.

Much of the time I act autonomously and independently. In fact, Jeff will agree that I am about the most independent woman he knows. But when we make major moves, and even some minor ones, and when I'm concerned about the children or my church assignments, or when I experience weakness and pain, I listen to and obey his counsel because I know he obeys our Father's counsel. I know that is the order of heaven.

If God created us to be one together, we must be number one for each other. "But from the beginning God made them male and female. For this cause shall a man leave his father and mother, and cleave to his wife; and they twain shall be one flesh." (Mark 10:6-8.)

I firmly believe that my husband comes first—before friends, father, mother, community, church, even children. We were together, alone, in the beginning of our marriage, and, heaven willing, we will be together in the end. Fortunately I think we have both been mature enough to realize when the children's needs have superseded our own, but our children now concede that the best thing we ever did for them, the greatest security they have enjoyed, was our loving of and caring for each other.

When our daughter, Mary, was about nine years old, she sensitively noticed that both Jeff and I were looking a little frazzled and frayed around the edges and so pronounced, "Mother, it's that time again. Take daddy and go away together." The children recognize that our time together is one of the most restoring, redeeming things we can do for them as well as for ourselves.

I love the Lord's injunction to Emma Smith—even to all wives: "The office of thy calling shall be for a comfort unto my servant, . . . thy husband, in his afflictions, with consoling words, in the spirit of meekness." (D&C 25:5.) I feel that I am at the pinnacle of my creation when I am comforting and consoling my husband. Nothing is more rewarding or brings me more joy. The sweetest sounds I hear are spoken when Jeff whispers to me, "You are my anchor, my foundation, my reassurance. I could never do this job without you."

And I love equally Paul's counsel to *all* husbands: "So ought men to love their wives as their own bodies. He that loveth his wife loveth himself, for no man ever yet hated his own flesh; but nourisheth and cherisheth it, even as the Lord the church: for we are members of his body, of his flesh, and of his bones." (Ephesians 5:28-30.)

Second, marriages are formed to procreate, to bring forth a posterity—having joy and rejoicing therein. A crucial part of any priority in a marriage, then, is children, even as I readily acknowledge that some couples have not been blessed with that opportunity. Indeed, most of my anxiety in life centers around my children. Since the world I live in is so full of complexities and challenges, I fear and tremble occasionally as I anticipate theirs. We are already seeing signs of their times. Enoch saw visions of their future; he saw their troubles and tribulations; he saw "men's hearts failing them, looking forth with fear." (See Moses 7:58-69.)

Jeff and I both agree that after our own effort toward individual and marital spirituality, our greatest spiritual priority is conscientious, devoted parenthood, to see that our children "shall not be afraid of evil tidings; [that their] hearts [are] fixed, trusting in the Lord." (Psalm 112:7.) We have

73

determined that our children will be peaceful, fixed, and trusting in the Lord—in large part at least—only so far as their parents are peaceful, fixed, and trusting in the Lord. I believe that the most powerful influence in a child's life is imitation, especially imitation of a parent. If we are hurried and worried or unbalanced in any way, surely our children will be hurried, worried, and unbalanced.

To live calmly and reassuringly for our children requires time—peaceful, loving, centered time. This means learning how to say no to some of the other demands that come along, without feeling guilty. I haven't learned yet how to do everything, but with the incredible practice I have had over the years, I have become an expert in saying no without feeling guilty. I receive one or two major speaking requests almost daily. But one person can do only so much. Jeff and I have counseled together, and we try to set aside appropriately proportioned time for ourselves, each other, our children, our church responsibilities, and our community. That is a lot to try to juggle.

So I have learned to say no to some things in order to be able to say yes to others. The most important yes we can say to our children is, "Yes, I have time for you." And for me that means both quantity and quality time.

I had two wonderful years serving full-time as a counselor in the Young Women's general presidency of the Church. For many reasons I am grateful the Lord called me out of the home for those two years of service. I was able to contribute to the lives of children who may not have the advantages we enjoy in our home. At the same time, my husband and children learned the importance of sacrifice and of serving each other, and the joy of knowing Christ will compensate and carry us when we are called according to his purposes.

Having a full-time opportunity outside of the home also taught me something of the challenges that are created when trying to juggle family and the expectations of the workplace. I am mindful of the tasks facing women who have to work while children are still at home. I certainly make no judgment nor wish to give offense over that difficult and sensitive matter. But I do know that through my experience, the Lord taught me valuable lessons about the needs of my children.

Contributing people, by their own success, work themselves into a position of more obligation. As my months of service continued, I began to see the mushrooming effect of those demands running headlong into my responsibilities as a wife and parent. As Deborah Fallows has written, "The more 'successful' the position is, in terms of prestige, power, money, and responsibility, the more commonplace and restricting its tyranny can be." (*A Mother's Work* [Boston: Houghton Mifflin, 1985], pp. 18-19.) In the workplace it is easier to ask our children to yield to the demands of our schedule rather than ask an employer to do so. Children haven't yet learned to speak up for their needs.

One afternoon my daughter, Mary, came home from school a little earlier than usual. Now if I had been in Salt Lake City, I wouldn't have been home to receive her, but that day the Lord positioned me where I was needed most. She entered the kitchen in tears about a conversation she had had with friends and a teacher over some controversial and disturbing issues. This led to the warmest, most intimate and enlightening experience we have ever had in her teen years, enough so that it prompted her to say, "You know, Mom, if you hadn't been home, we never would have had this conversation because I wouldn't have felt the need after a peanut butter sandwich and a little TV."

Since the conversation had to do with virtues and values that are incredibly important, I have thanked the Lord frequently for just that one moment. Our best quality moments with our children often come *not* when we're prepared and trying to have them, but as surprising, fleeting episodes that we couldn't have anticipated. If we are lucky, we are there to catch those moments.

Being away from my children for long hours over two

years helped me to understand that when one or more of my children are overwhelmed or confused or struggling, there is a distinct way that I will respond as their mother—different from how a babysitter, friend, or even their grandmother, however loving or confident she may be, would respond. Ironically, it was through my full-time service to a church program that I learned fully to appreciate that no one else can mother my children as well as I can, and that my greatest task and joy is as a wife and mother in my own home.

Deborah Fallows sums up my feelings exactly: "To meet my standard of responsible parenthood, I have to know [my children] as well as I possibly can and see them in as many different environments and moods as possible in order to know best how to help them grow up, by comforting them, letting them alone, disciplining them, enjoying them, being dependable but not stifling. What I need is *time* with them—in quantity, not [just] 'quality.' " (Ibid., p. 16.)

Noted psychologist Scott Peck has written: "The parents who devote time to their children even when it is not demanded by glaring misdeeds will perceive in them subtle needs for discipline, to which they will respond with gentle urging or reprimand or structure or praise, administered with thoughtfulness and care. They will observe how their children eat cake, how they study, when they tell subtle falsehoods, when they run away from problems rather than face them. They will take the time to make these minor corrections and adjustments, listening to their children, responding to them, tightening a little here, loosening a little there, giving them little lectures, little stories, little hugs and kisses, little admonishments, little pats on the back." *(The Road Less Traveled* [New York: Touchstone, 1978], p. 23.)

Essential to every child's mental health is the feeling, "I am valuable." And where we choose to spend our time reveals to our children exactly how valuable they are. In this way, children provide parents their greatest spiritual development. Our children are our practice in being eternal parents.

The final priority in our spirituality has to do with building the kingdom of God. I always try to remember that all of our major priorities are related, that the Church is an earthly structure provided to help me in my eternal responsibility to my God, my family, and those others upon whom I can have righteous influence, living or dead. The Church helps me so much in those tasks that I am more than willing to take my turn, to play my part in helping others in their progress.

Of course, the Lord knows that our church service, besides blessing and helping others, increases our own personal development. I fully acknowledge that because of my church service, I have begun to develop talents I wasn't sure were there — talents of speaking, writing, teaching, music, learning, and especially loving. Above all, the Church provides a structure for developing my Godly attribute of charity.

Sometimes choosing between family and church is the most difficult of all the choices we face. But here, too, our prophets have given guidelines for deciding what is essential and what is secondary. When every home is patterned after the order of the temple — "even a house of prayer, a house of fasting, a house of faith, a house of learning, a house of glory, a house of order, a house of God" (D&C 109:8) — the kingdom of God will come. But since neither we nor our homes are yet perfect, and because many are yet pioneering with less privilege than some others have had, we extend ourselves through the structure and programs of the Church to teach, bless, serve, and sacrifice for others who are not in our own family until we are equal in all things. We are all blessed immeasurably for our service in the Church. It is the most beneficial way we have to keep the two great commandments: to love God and our neighbors as we love ourselves.

Let me end just as I began, by coming full circle. In a very personal way I have shared my perspective of the organization and order that the teachings of the temple have provided for me, but not with the idea that your life should be exactly like Pat Holland's, for each of us will have peace only as we are

77

filling the measure of our *own* creation. My prayer is merely that I have been able to trigger your thought processes for establishing priorities for your own life. My hope is that this message will create in each of us a desire to mentally mark out our purpose in life so that we will not fall easy prey to petty worries, fears, and weaknesses, or to temporary failures, setbacks, and unhappiness. You see, like you, I have those wonderful days when I wake up feeling warm, cozy, with feelings of purpose and peace that all is well. But dynamic tensions are at work in each of us. Burdens of mystery, divine discontent, and inner turmoil keep us from complacency, creating Christlike energy searching for new truth.

On those days when I feel off center, out of focus, or off balance, when I feel that I don't have enough time, insight, or strength to solve my problems, I know that comfort is as close as the temple. Before I go to the temple, I retreat to a private room in my home, one where, from frequent prayer, I feel I have come closest to my Father in heaven. There I kneel and express my deepest feelings of love and gratitude. I also pour out my troubles to him one by one by one, laying every burden and placing every decision at the Lord's feet. Thus prepared, I then take myself out of this world of fashion, frenzy, and occasional phoniness and go the House of the Lord. There, dressed like my neighbor, and with no windows and no clocks to distract me, I am able to see this world objectively. There I remember that the whole of this life is a journey of the spirit to a higher and holier sphere. I remember that the success of my journey depends on my adherence to the sequential steps God has put on my individual road map.

While serving another sister in the temple, someone who didn't have my privileges during her lifetime, I have time for solitude, private prayer, and meditation. I have time to listen and to contemplate the steps I can take, those steps that are right for me. The Lord often shows me how to effectively make choices between right and wrong—and between right and right. He blesses me to see what is essential and what is secondary. I feel comforted regarding my discouragements, and I am able to see those moments as merely messages guiding me back toward my own individual divine destiny. If the Lord in his love and graciousness does that for me, I bear you my testimony that he will also do that for you!

We are children of heavenly parents who have invited us on a journey to become like them. They have provided for us, just a shadow away, a sacred home where we can go and remember that there is joy in this journey, that our paths do have a purpose, and that life can be lived as lovingly on earth as it is in heaven. May all of our faces—our many faces of Eve—reflect the radiant spirit of the Lord and the great glory of God which is ours.

Chapter 8

WITH YOUR
FACE TO THE SON

*All of us are Eve's daughters, whether we are married
or single, maternal or barren. We are created in the image
of God to become goddesses. And we can provide something of that maternal prototype for each other and those
who come after us. Whatever our circumstance, we can
reach out, touch, hold, lift, and nurture—but we cannot
do it in isolation. We need a community of sisters stilling
the soul and binding the wounds of fragmentation.*

Just after my release from the Young Women general
presidency in April 1986, I had the opportunity of spending a week in Israel. It had been a very difficult and demanding two years for me. Being a good mother with ample
time to succeed at that task has always been my first priority,
so I had tried to be a full-time mother to a grade-schooler, a
high-schooler, and a son preparing for his mission. I had also
tried to be a full-time wife to a staggeringly busy university
president. And I had to be as much of a full-time counselor
in that general presidency as one living fifty miles from the
office could be. But in an important period of forming principles and starting programs, I worried that I wasn't doing
enough—and I tried to run a little faster.

Toward the end of my two-year term, my health was going
downhill. I was losing weight steadily, and I wasn't sleeping
well. My husband and children were trying to bandage me
together even as I was trying to do the same for them. We

were exhausted. And yet, I kept wondering what I might have done to manage it all better. The Brethren, always compassionate, were watching, and extended a loving release. As grateful as my family and I were for the conclusion of my term of service, I nevertheless felt a loss of association—and, I confess, some loss of identity—with these women whom I had come to love so much. Who was I, and where was I in this welter of demands? Should life be as hard as all this? How successful had I been in my several and competing assignments? Or had I muffed them all? The days after my release were about as difficult as the weeks before it. I didn't have any reserve to call on. My tank was on empty, and I wasn't sure there was a filling station anywhere in sight.

Just a few weeks later my husband had an assignment in Jerusalem, and the Brethren traveling on the assignment requested that I accompany him. "Come on," he said. "You can recuperate in the Savior's land of living water and bread of life." As weary as I was, I packed my bags, believing—or, at the very least, hoping—that the time there would be a healing respite.

On a pristinely clear and beautifully bright day, I sat overlooking the Sea of Galilee and reread the tenth chapter of Luke. But instead of the words on the page, I thought I saw with my mind and heard with my heart these words: "[Pat, Pat, Pat,] thou art careful and troubled about many things." Then the power of pure and personal revelation seized me as I read, "But one thing—only one thing—is truly needful." (See Luke 10:40-41.)

The May sun in Israel is so bright that you feel as if you are sitting on top of the world. I had just visited the spot in Bethoron where the sun stood still for Joshua (see Joshua 10:12), and indeed, on that day it seemed so for me as well. As I sat pondering my problems, I felt that same sun's healing rays like warm liquid pouring into my heart, relaxing, calming, and comforting my troubled soul.

Our loving Father in heaven seemed to be whispering to

81

me, "You don't have to worry over so many things. The one thing that is needful—the *only* thing that is truly needful—is to keep your eyes toward the sun—my Son." Suddenly I had true peace. I knew that my life had always been in his hands, from the very beginning! The sea lying peacefully before my eyes had been tempest-tossed and dangerous—many, many times. All I needed to do was to renew my faith and get a firm grasp of his hand, and *together* we could walk on the water.

I would like to pose a question for each of us to ponder. How do we as women make that quantum leap from being troubled and worried, including worried about legitimate concerns, to being women of even greater faith? One frame of mind surely seems to negate the other. Faith and fear cannot long coexist. Consider some of the things that trouble us.

I have served as a Relief Society president in four different wards. Two of these wards were for single women and two were wards with many young mothers. As I sat in counsel with my single sisters, my heart often ached as they described to me their feelings of loneliness and disappointment. They felt that their lives had no meaning or purpose in a church that, rightly, puts so much emphasis on marriage and family life. Most painful of all was the occasional suggestion that their singleness was their own fault—or worse yet, a selfish desire. They were anxiously seeking for peace and purpose, something of real value to which they could dedicate their lives.

Yet it seemed to me that the young mothers had easily as many concerns. They described to me the struggles of trying to raise children in an increasingly difficult world, of never having enough time or means or freedom to feel like a person of value because they were always stretched to the ragged edge of survival. And there were so few tangible evidences that what they were doing was really going to be successful. There was no one to give them a raise in pay, and, beyond their husbands (who might or might not remember to do it), no one to compliment them on a job well done. And they were always tired! The one thing I remember so vividly with these young mothers is that they were always so tired.

Then there were those women who, through no fault of their own, found themselves the sole provider for their homes financially, spiritually, emotionally, and in every other way. I could not even comprehend the challenges they faced. Obviously, in some ways, theirs was the most demanding circumstance of all.

The perspective I have gained over these many years of listening to the worries of women is that no one woman or group of women—single, married, divorced, widowed, homemakers, or professionals—has cornered the full market on concerns. There seem to be plenty of challenges to go around.

Every one of us has privileges and blessings, and every one of us has fears and trials. It seems bold to say, but common sense suggests that never before in the history of the world have women, including Latter-day Saint women, been faced with greater complexity in their concerns.

I am very appreciative of the added awareness that the women's movement has given to a gospel principle we have had since Mother Eve and before—that of agency, the right to choose. But one of the most unfortunate side effects we have faced in this matter of agency is that, because of the increasing diversity of life-styles for women of today, we seem even more uncertain and less secure with each other. We are not getting closer, but further away from that sense of community and sisterhood that has sustained us and given us strength for generations. There seems to be an increase in our competitiveness and a decrease in our generosity with one another.

Those who have the time and energy to can their fruit and vegetables develop a great skill that will serve them well in time of need—and in our economy, that could be almost anytime. But they shouldn't look down their noses at those who buy their peaches, or who don't like zucchini in any of the thirty-five ways there are to disguise it, or who have simply made a conscious choice to use their time and energy in some other purposeful ways.

And where am I in all of this? For three-fourths of my life I felt threatened to the core because I hated to sew. Now, I *can* sew; if it is absolutely necessary, I *will* sew — but I hate it. Can you imagine my burden over the last twenty-five or thirty years, "faking it" in Relief Society meetings and trying to smile when six little girls walk into church all pinafored and laced and ribboned and petticoated, wearing identical, hand-sewn dresses, all trooping ahead of their mother, who has a similar outfit? I don't necessarily consider my attitude virtuous, lovely, of good report, or praiseworthy, but I'm honest in my antipathy toward sewing.

I have grown up a little since those days in at least two ways: I now genuinely admire a mother who can do that for her children, and I have ceased feeling guilty that sewing is not particularly rewarding to me. The point is, we simply cannot call ourselves Christian and continue to judge one another — or ourselves — so harshly. No jar of bing cherries is worth a confrontation that robs us of our compassion and our sisterhood.

Obviously the Lord has created us with different personalities, as well as differing degrees of energy, interest, health, talent, and opportunity. So long as we are committed to righteousness and living a life of faithful devotion, we should celebrate these divine differences, knowing they are a gift from God. We must not feel so frightened, so threatened and insecure; we must not need to find exact replicas of ourselves in order to feel validated as women of worth. There are many things over which we can be divided, but *one* thing is needful for our unity: the empathy and compassion of the living Son of God.

I was married in 1963, the very year Betty Friedan published her society-shaking book, *The Feminine Mystique*, so as an adult woman I can only look back with childhood memories of the gentler 1940s and '50s. But it must have been much more comfortable to have a life-style already prepared for you, and neighbors on either side whose lives gave you role models for your own. However, it must have been even that much more painful for those who, through no fault of their own, were single then, or had to work, or struggled with broken families. Now, in our increasingly complex world, that earlier model is fragmented, and we seem to be even less sure of who we are and where we are going.

Surely there has not been another time in history when women have questioned their self-worth so harshly and critically as in the second half of the twentieth century. Many women are searching, almost frantically, as never before, for a sense of personal purpose and meaning; and many LDS women are searching too, for eternal insight and meaning in their femaleness.

If I were Satan and wanted to destroy a society, I think I would stage a full-blown blitz on women. I would keep them so distraught and distracted that they would never find the calming strength and serenity for which their gender has always been known.

Satan has effectively done that, catching us in the crunch of trying to be superhuman instead of striving to reach our unique, God-given potential within such diversity. He tauntingly teases us that if we don't have it all—fame, fortune, families, and fun—and have it every minute all the time, we have been shortchanged and are second-class citizens in the race of life. As women, we are struggling, our families are struggling, and our society is struggling. Drugs, teenage pregnancies, divorce, family violence, and suicide are some of the ever-increasing side effects of our collective life in the express lane.

Too many of us are struggling and suffering, too many are running faster than they have strength, expecting too much of themselves. As a result, we are experiencing new and undiagnosed stress-related illnesses. The Epstein-Barr virus, for one, has come into our popular medical jargon as the malady of the 1980s. The victims "are plagued by low-grade fevers, aching joints, and sometimes a sore throat—but they don't have the flu. They're overwhelmingly exhausted, weak, and debilitated—but they don't have AIDS. They're often confused and forgetful—but it isn't Alzheimer's. Many patients feel suicidal, but it isn't clinical depression. . . . Female victims outnumber males about 3 to 1, and a great many are intelligent high achievers with stressful lives." (*Newsweek*, October 27, 1986, p. 105.)

We *must* have the courage to be imperfect while striving for perfection. We *must* not allow our own guilt, or the feminist books, the talk-show hosts, or the whole media culture to sell us a bill of goods—or rather a bill of *no* goods. We can become so sidetracked in our compulsive search for identity and self-esteem that we really believe it can be found in having perfect figures or academic degrees or professional status or even absolute motherly success. Yet, in so searching externally, we can be torn from our true internal, eternal selves. We often worry so much about pleasing and performing for others that we lose our own uniqueness—that full and relaxed acceptance of one's self as a person of worth and individuality. We become so frightened and insecure that we cannot be generous toward the diversity and individuality and, yes, problems, of our neighbors. Too many women with these anxieties watch helplessly as their lives unravel from the very core that centers and sustains them. Too many are like a ship at sea without sail or rudder, "tossed to and fro," as the Apostle Paul said (see Ephesians 4:14), until more and more of us are genuinely, rail-grabbingly seasick.

Where is the sureness that allows us to sail our ship whatever winds may blow, with the master seaman's triumphant cry, "Steady as she goes"? Where is the inner stillness we so cherish and for which women have traditionally been known?

I believe we can find our steady footing and stilling of the soul by turning away from physical preoccupations, super-woman accomplishments, and endless popularity contests, and returning instead to the wholeness of our soul, that unity in our very being that balances the demanding and inevitable diversity of life.

One woman, not of our faith, whose writings I love is Anne Morrow Lindbergh. She comments on the female despair and general torment of our times:

"The Feminists did not look . . . far [enough] ahead; they laid down no rules of conduct. For them it was enough to demand the privileges. . . . And [so] woman today is still searching. We are aware of our hunger and needs, but still ignorant of what will satisfy them. With our garnered free time, we are more apt to drain our creative springs than to refill them. With our pitchers we attempt . . . to water a field, [instead of] a garden. We throw ourselves indiscriminately into committees and cause. Not knowing how to feed the spirit, we try to muffle its demands in distractions. Instead of stilling the center, the axis of the wheel, we add more centrifugal activities to our lives—which tend to throw us off balance. Mechanically we have gained, in the last generation, but spiritually we have . . . lost." Regardless of the time period, she adds, for women "the problem is [still] how to feed the soul." (Anne Morrow Lindbergh, *Gift from the Sea* [New York: Pantheon Books, 1975], pp. 51-52.)

I have pondered long and hard about the feeding of our inner self, of the "one thing needful" amidst too many troublesome things. It is no coincidence that we speak of feeding the spirit, just as we would speak of feeding the body. We need constant nourishment for both. The root word *hale* (as in "hale and hearty") is the common root to words like *whole, health, heal,* and *holy.* President Ezra Taft Benson recently said, "There is no question that the health of the body affects the spirit, or the Lord would never have revealed the Word of Wisdom. God has never given any *temporal* commandments—and that which affects our stature affects our soul." We need so much for body, mind, and spirit to unite in one healthy, stable soul.

Surely God is well balanced, so perhaps we are just that much closer to him when *we* are. In any case, I like the link between *hale, whole, health, heal,* and *holy.* Our unity of soul within diversity of circumstance—our "stilling of the center"—is worth any effort.

Often we fail to consider the glorious possibility within our own souls. We need to remember that divine promise, "The kingdom of God is within you." (Luke 17:21.) Perhaps we forget that the kingdom of God is within us because too much attention is given to this outer shell, this human body of ours, and the frail, too-flimsy world in which it moves.

Permit me to share with you an analogy that I created from something I read years ago. It helped me then, and helps me still, in my examination of inner strength and spiritual growth.

The analogy is of a soul—a human soul, with all of its splendor—being placed in a beautifully carved but very tightly locked box. Reigning in majesty and illuminating our soul in this innermost box is our Lord and our Redeemer, Jesus Christ, the living Son of the living God. This box is then placed—and locked—inside another larger one, and so on until five beautifully carved but very securely locked boxes await the woman who is skillful and wise enough to open them. In order for her to have free communication with the Lord, she must find the key to and unlock the contents of these boxes. Success will then reveal to her the beauty and divinity of her own soul and her gifts and her grace as a daughter of God.

For me, prayer is the key to the first box. We kneel to ask help for the tasks and then arise to find that the first lock is now open. But this ought not to seem just a convenient and contrived miracle, for if we are to search for real light and eternal certainties, we have to pray as the ancients prayed. We are women now, not children, and are expected to pray with maturity. The words most often used to describe urgent, prayerful labor are *wrestle, plead, cry,* and *hunger.* In some sense, prayer may be the hardest work we will ever be engaged in, and perhaps it should be. It is pivotal protection against becoming so involved with worldly possessions and honors and status that we no longer desire to undertake the search for our soul.

Those who, like Enos, pray in faith and gain entrance to a new dimension of their divinity are led to box number two. Here our prayers alone do not seem to be sufficient. We must turn to the scriptures for God's long-recorded teachings about our soul. We must learn. Surely every woman in the Church is under divine obligation to learn and grow and develop. We are God's diverse array of unburnished talents, and we must not bury these gifts nor hide our light. If the glory of God is intelligence, then learning, especially learning from the scriptures, stretches us toward him.

He uses many metaphors for divine influence such as "living water" and "the bread of life." I have discovered that if my own progress stalls, it stalls from malnutrition born of not eating and drinking daily from his holy writ. There have been challenges in my life that would have completely destroyed me had I not had the scriptures both on my bedstand and in my purse so that I could partake of them day and night at a moment's notice. Meeting God in scripture has been like a divine intravenous feeding for me—a celestial I.V. that my son once described as an "angelical" cord. So box two is opened through learning from the scriptures. I have discovered that by studying them I can have, again and again, an exhilarating encounter with God.

However, at the beginning of such success in emancipating the soul, Lucifer becomes more anxious, especially as we approach box number three. He knows that we are about to learn one very important and fundamental principle—that to truly find ourselves we must lose ourselves—so he begins to block our increased efforts to love God, love our neighbor, and love ourselves. Through the last decade, Satan has enticed all humanity to engage almost all of their energies in the pursuit of romantic love or thing-love or excessive self-love. In so doing, we forget that appropriate self-love and self-esteem are the promised reward for putting others first. "Whosoever shall seek to save his life shall lose it; and whosoever shall lose his life shall preserve it." (Luke 17:33.) Thus, box three opens only to the key of charity.

With charity, real growth and genuine insight begin. But the lid to box four seems nearly impossible to penetrate. Unfortunately, the fainthearted and fearful often turn back here. The going seems too difficult, the lock too secure. This is a time for self-evaluation. To see ourselves as we really are often brings pain, but it is only through true humility, repentance, and renewal that we will come to know God. "Learn of me; for I am meek and lowly in heart," he said. (Matthew 11:29.)

We must be patient with ourselves as we overcome weaknesses, and we must remember to rejoice over all that is good in us. This will strengthen our inner selves and leave us less dependent on outward acclaim. When our souls pay less attention to public praise, they then also care very little about public disapproval. Competition and jealousy and now envy begin to have no meaning. Just imagine the powerful spirit that would exist in our female society if we finally arrived at the point where, like our Savior, our real desire was to be counted as the *least* among our sisters. The rewards here are of such profound strength and quiet triumph of faith that we are carried into an even brighter sphere. So the fourth box, unlike the others, is broken open, just as a contrite heart is broken. We are reborn, like a flower growing and blooming out of the broken crust of the earth.

To share with you my feelings of opening the fifth box, I must compare the beauty of our souls with the holiness of our temples. There, in a setting not of this world, where fashions and position and professions go unrecognized, we have our opportunity to find peace and serenity and stillness that will anchor our soul forever, for there we may find God. For those of us who, like the brother of Jared, have the courage and faith to break through the veil into that sacred center of existence, we will find the brightness of the final box brighter than the noonday sun. There we find wholeness—holiness. That is what it says over the entrance to the fifth box: Holiness to the Lord. "Know ye not that ye are the temple of God?" (1 Corinthians 3:16.) I testify that each of us is holy—that divinity is abiding within us waiting to be uncovered—to be unleashed and magnified and demonstrated.

I have heard it said by some that the reason women in the Church struggle somewhat to know themselves is because they don't have a divine female role model. But we do. We believe we have a mother in heaven. President Spencer W. Kimball declared in a general conference address: "When we sing that doctrinal hymn . . . 'O My Father,' we get a sense of the ultimate in maternal modesty, of the restrained, queenly elegance of our heavenly mother, and, knowing how profoundly our mortal mothers have shaped us here, do we suppose her influence on us as individuals to be less?" (*Ensign*, May 1978, p. 4.)

I have never questioned why our mother in heaven seems veiled to us, for I believe the Lord has his reasons for revealing as little as he has on that subject. Furthermore, I believe we know much more about our eternal nature than we think we do; and it is our sacred obligation to express our knowledge, to teach it to our young sisters and daughters, and in so doing to strengthen their faith and help them through the counterfeit confusions of these difficult latter days. Let me point out some examples.

The Lord has not placed us in this lone and dreary world without a blueprint for living. In the Doctrine and Covenants we read the Lord's words: "I will give unto you a pattern in all things, that ye may not be deceived." (D&C 52:14.) He certainly includes women in that promise. He has given us patterns in the Bible, the Book of Mormon, the Doctrine and

Covenants, and the Pearl of Great Price, and he has given us patterns in the temple ceremony. As we study these patterns we must continually ask, "Why does the Lord choose to say these particular words and present them in just this way?" We know he uses metaphors and symbols and parables and allegories to teach us of his eternal ways. We have all recognized the relationship between Abraham and Isaac that so parallels God's anguish over the sacrifice of his own Son, Jesus Christ. But, as women, do we stretch ourselves and also ask about Sarah's travail in this experience as well? We need to search in this manner, and we need to look always for deeper meaning. We should look for parallels and symbols. We should look for themes and motifs such as those we would find in a Bach or a Mozart composition, and we should look for repeated patterns.

One obvious pattern is that both the Bible and the Book of Mormon begin with a family theme, including family conflict. I have always believed this symbolized something eternal about family far more than just the story of those particular parents or those particular children. Surely all of us — married or single, with children and without — see something of Adam and Eve and something of Cain and Abel every day of our lives. With or without marriage, or with or without children, we all have some of the feelings of Lehi, Sariah, Laman, Nephi, Ruth, Naomi, Esther, the sons of Helaman, and the daughters of Ishmael.

Those are types and shadows for us, prefigurations of our own mortal joys and sorrows, just as Joseph and Mary are, in a sense, types and shadows of parental devotion as they nurtured the Son of God. These all seem to me to be symbols of higher principles and truths, symbols carefully chosen to show us the way, whether we are married or single, young or old, with family or without.

And, obviously, the temple is highly symbolic. May I share an experience I had there a few months ago concerning the careful choice of words and symbols? I have chosen my own words carefully so that nothing will be improperly shared outside the temple. My quotations are taken from published scripture.

Maybe it was coincidence (someone has said that "coincidence is a small miracle in which God chooses to remain anonymous"), but in any case, as I waited in the temple chapel, I sat next to a very elderly man who unexpectedly but sweetly turned to me and said, "If you want a clear picture of the Creation, read Abraham 4." As I started to turn to Abraham, I just happened to brush past Moses 3:5: "For I, the Lord God, created all things, of which I have spoken, spiritually, before they were naturally upon the face of the earth." Another message of prefiguration — a spiritual pattern giving meaning to mortal creations. I then read Abraham 4 carefully and took the opportunity of going to an initiatory session. I left there with greater revelatory light on something I had always known in my heart to be so — that men *and* women are joint heirs of the blessings of the priesthood, and even though men bear the greater burden of administering it, women are not without their priesthood-related responsibilities.

Then, as I attended the endowment session, I asked myself: If I were the Lord and could only give my children on earth a simplified but powerfully symbolic example of their roles and missions, how much would I give and where would I start? I listened to every word. I watched for patterns and prototypes.

I quote to you from Abraham 4:27: "So the Gods went down to organize man in their own image, in the image of the Gods to form they him, male *and* female, to form they *them*." (Italics added.) They formed male and they formed female — in the image of the Gods, in *their* own image.

Then, in a poignant exchange with God, Adam states that he will call the woman Eve. And why does he call her Eve? "Because she [is] the mother of all living." (Genesis 3:20; Moses 4:26.)

93

As I tenderly acknowledge the very real pain that many single women, or married women who have not borne children, feel about any discussion of motherhood, could we consider this one possibility about our eternal female identity—our unity in our diversity? Eve was given the identity of "the mother of all living"—years, decades, perhaps centuries before she ever bore a child. It would appear that her motherhood preceded her maternity, just as surely as the perfection of the Garden preceded the struggles of mortality. I believe *mother* is one of those very carefully chosen words, one of those rich words, with meaning after meaning after meaning. We must not, at all costs, let that word divide us. I believe with all my heart that it is first and foremost a statement about our nature, not a head count of our children.

I have only three children and have wept that I could not have more. And I know that some women without any have wept too. And sometimes too, many have simply been angry over the very subject itself. For the sake of our eternal motherhood, I plead that this not be so. Some women give birth and raise children but never "mother" them. Others, whom I love with all my heart, "mother" all their lives but have never given birth. All of us are Eve's daughters, whether we are married or single, maternal or barren; and we can provide something of that divine pattern, that maternal prototype, for each other and for those who come after us. Whatever our circumstances, we can reach out, touch, hold, lift, and nurture, but we cannot do it in isolation. We need a community of sisters stilling the soul and binding the wounds of fragmentation.

I know that God loves us individually and collectively as women, and that he has a mission for every one of us. As I learned on my Galilean hillside, I testify that if our desires are righteous, God overrules for our good and that heavenly parents will tenderly attend to our needs. In our diversity and individuality, my prayer is that we will be united—united in seeking our specific, foreordained mission, united in asking not, "What can the kingdom do for me?" but "What can I do for the kingdom? How do I fulfill the measure of my creation? In my circumstances and my challenges and with my faith, where is my full realization of the Godly image in which I was created?"

With faith in God, his prophets, his church, and ourselves—with faith in our own divine creation—may we be peaceful and let go of our cares and troubles over so many things. May we believe, nothing doubting, in the light that shines, even in a dark place.

A CONVERSATION

with Jeffrey R. Holland
and Patricia T. Holland

Chapter 9

SOME
THINGS WE HAVE
LEARNED – TOGETHER

*Marriage is the highest and holiest of all human rela-
tionships – or at least it ought to be. It offers never-ending
opportunities for the practice of every Christian virtue
and for the demonstration of truly divine love. By the
same token, marriage can also be the setting for struggle
and difficulty, especially if husband and wife do not work
as one. This discussion, delivered in 1983, is as we
presented it – together.*

JRH: This year we reach a milestone in our lives: we will
have lived as long married to each other, twenty-two years,
as we did before marriage. Surely that ought to justify some
sort of sage advice from us. I was told on that fateful day in
1963 that with marriage I had come to the end of my troubles.
I just didn't realize which end they were speaking of.

PTH: The last thing we want to do is sound self-righteous,
so our first assurance is that our marriage is not perfect, and
we have the scar tissue to prove it. To quote my father, the
rocks in Jeff's head have not yet filled the holes in mine.

JRH: So forgive us for using the only marriage we know,
imperfect as it is, but for some time now we have wanted to
reflect back on the half of our lives spent together since we
were students at BYU and to see what, if anything, it might
mean twenty-two years from now.

PTH: Let me reassure you that this isn't going to be the
usual talk on matrimony. For one thing, we are going to try

99

to apply these little lessons we have learned to everyone, single or married. For another thing, we fear that too many, especially women, are too anxious about the subject already. So please don't be anxious.

JRH: On the other hand, I know a few men who ought to be a little more anxious than they are. Men, get anxious. Or to be slightly more scriptural, get "anxiously engaged."

PTH: We really believe that romance and marriage, if they are going to come, will come a lot more naturally if young people worry about them a lot less. By the same token, we also know that this is easy to say and hard to do. It's hard because so much of our young life in the Church is measured on a precise time sequence. We are baptized at eight. At twelve young men are ordained deacons and young women enter Mutual. Then we date at sixteen, graduate from high school at eighteen, and go on missions at nineteen or twenty-one.

JRH: But then, suddenly, it is less and less structured, less and less certain. When do we marry? Surely in a Church manual somewhere there must be a specific year for that! Well, there isn't. Matters of marriage are much more personal than a prepublished celestial calendar would allow. And so our anxiety level leaps.

PTH: With that acknowledgment, we are aware that some will not marry during their college years, nor perhaps during the years thereafter. By talking on this subject, we do not intend to make it more painful for some than it already is, but rather to draw some observations from our own marriage that might be of value to all—younger, older, married, or single. We pray for the blessings of the Lord to help us share something of our brief, ordinary, and sometimes tumultuous life together. Another twenty-two years of working things out would let us give a much better talk.

JRH: With that long introduction, I don't know whether this is our first piece of counsel or our last, but in any case, don't rush things needlessly and unnaturally. Nature has its rhythms and its harmonies. We would do well to fit ourselves

100

as best we can with those cycles rather than frantically throwing ourselves against them.

PTH: As we look back on it now, twenty-two seems, if anything, pretty young to be getting married, though that was the right time for us. When it is right, it should be pursued, and for some that will be younger—or older—than for others. But don't march to an arbitrary drummer who seems to be beating a frenzied candence to the passing years.

JRH: Twenty-one—

PTH: (Oh, dear, I'm facing . . .)

JRH: Twenty-two—

PTH: (Will I ever find him?)

JRH: Twenty-three—

PTH: (Oh, woe is me, woe is me.)

JRH: Twenty-four—

PTH: (Death, make me thine! O grave, receive me!)

JRH: Well, that's a little melodramatic, but not much.

PTH: We know of a few—not many, but a few—who have panicked that she . . .

JRH: or he . . .

PTH: has not yet hit that matrimonial target established at ten years of age, or, worse yet, one established by a well-meaning aunt whose greeting every Christmas seems to be, "Well, you've been at BYU a full semester now. Have you found Mr. Right?"

JRH: Or that solicitous uncle who says, "You've been home from your mission six weeks now. I guess wedding bells will be ringing soon, won't they? *They will, won't they?*"

PTH: Of course, we are not the best ones in the world to speak on that particular aspect, inasmuch as we were engaged thirty days after Jeff got home from his mission.

JRH: Well, I had a solicitous uncle.

PTH: But you also have to remember that we knew each other well for two years before we started dating, dated another two years before Jeff's mission, and then wrote for those two years he was away. That's six years of friendship before

101

we were engaged. Besides, when I first dated Jeff I couldn't stand him. (I just throw that in as reassurance to women who are dating men they can't stand.)

JRH: I let her throw it in as reassurance to the men who can't be stood!

PTH: Then, still not to be outdone in the waiting game, I left for New York the day after we were engaged, leaving Jeff to hammer away at school while I studied music and filled a stake mission three-fourths of a continent away from him. That added another ten months, so I think it's fair to say we didn't rush things.

JRH: Quite apart from the matter of school or missions or marriage or whatever, life ought to be enjoyed at every stage of our experience and should not be hurried and wrenched and truncated and torn to fit an unnatural schedule we have predetermined but that may not be the Lord's personal plan for us at all. As we look back today, we realize we have probably rushed too many things and been too anxious and too urgent for too much of our life, and perhaps you are already guilty of the same thing. We probably all get caught thinking real life is still ahead of us, still a little farther down the road.

PTH: Don't wait to live. Obviously, life for all of us began a long time ago—twenty-two years longer for us than for you—and the sand is falling through that hourglass as steadily as the sun rises and rivers run to the sea. Don't wait for life to gallop in and sweep you off your feet. It is a quieter, more pedestrian visitor than that. In a church that understands more about time and its relationship to eternity than any other, we of all people ought to savor every moment, ought to enjoy the time of preparation *before* marriage, filling it full of all the truly good things of life—one of the most valuable of which is a university education.

JRH: Let me add just one other related caution. In my professional and ecclesiastical life working with young adults—roughly the same second-half period of my life that corresponds to our marriage — I have regularly run into young men and women who are looking for that idealized partner who is some perfect amalgamation of virtues and character- istics seen in parents, loved ones, church leaders, movie stars, sports heroes, political leaders, or any other wonderful men and women we may have known.

PTH: Certainly it is important to have thought through those qualities and attributes that you most admire in others, and that you yourself ought to be acquiring. But remember that when young people have visited with Sister Camilla Kim- ball about how wonderful it must be to be married to a prophet, she has said, "Yes, it is wonderful to be married to a prophet, but I didn't marry a prophet. I just married a returned missionary." Consider this statement from President Kimball on such down-to-earth choices:

JRH: "Two people coming from difference backgrounds soon learn after the ceremony is performed that stark reality must be faced. There is no longer a life of fantasy or of make- believe; we must come out of the clouds and put our feet firmly on the earth. . . .

"One comes to realize very soon after the marriage that the spouse has weaknesses not previously revealed or dis- covered. The virtues that were constantly magnified during courtship now grow relatively smaller, and the weaknesses that seemed so small and insignificant during courtship now grow to sizeable proportions. . . . Yet real, lasting happiness is possible. . . . [It] is within the reach of every couple, every person. 'Soulmates' are fiction and an illusion; and while every young man and young woman will seek with all diligence and prayerfulness to find a mate with whom life can be most compatible and beautiful, yet it is certain that almost any good man and any good woman can have happiness and a suc- cessful marriage if both are willing to pay the price." (*Marriage and Divorce* [Salt Lake City: Deseret Book, 1976], pp. 13, 18.)

PTH: On that note, let us share with you a little "stark reality" of our own. Jeff and I have conversations from time to time that bring us down "out of the clouds," to use President Kimball's phrase. Do you want to know what I have told him he does that irritates me the most? It is that he walks everywhere in a hurry—first five, then ten, then fifty feet in front of me. I have learned now to just call out and tell him to save me a place when he gets where he's going.

JRH: Well, as long as we are telling secrets, do you want to know what irritates me? It is that she is always late and that we are therefore always running to get somewhere, with me first five, then ten, then fifty feet in front of her.

PTH: We have learned to laugh about that a little, and now compromise. I watch the time a bit better, he slows down a stride or two, and we actually touch fingertips about every other bounce.

JRH: But we don't have everything worked out yet—like room temperatures. I used to joke about LDS scripturalists who worried about the body temperature of translated beings. I don't joke anymore, because I now worry seriously about my wife's body temperature. She has an electric blanket on high for eleven months of the year. She suffers hypothermia at the Fourth of July picnic. She thaws out from about 2:00 to 3:30 on the afternoon of August 12; then it's bundle-up time again.

PTH: He ought to talk. He throws the window open every night as if he's Admiral Peary looking for the North Pole. But just let someone suggest a little winter morning's jogging and he sounds like a wounded Siberian sheepdog. Mr. Health here can't tie his shoelaces without taking oxygen.

JRH: As for different backgrounds, it's hard to think two kids from St. George could have different backgrounds—or even any background at all. But regarding financial matters, Pat came from a family in which her father was very careful with money (and therefore always had some to share generously) while my dad grew up without any money but later spent it as generously as if he had. Both families were very happy, but when the two of us came together it was "Hail, Columbia . . ."

PTH: " . . . and the devil take the hindmost." That introduces to us another of those "stark realities" of marriage. To quote Elder Marvin J. Ashton in an address to the membership of the Church:

"How important are money management and finances in marriage and family affairs? Tremendously. The American Bar Association recently indicated that 89 percent of all divorces could be traced to quarrels and accusations over money. [Another study] estimated that 75 percent of all divorces result from clashes over finances. Some professional counselors indicate that four out of [every] five families [wrestle] with serious money problems. . . . A prospective wife could well concern herself not with the amount her husband-to-be can earn in a month, but rather how will he manage the money that comes into his hands. . . . A prospective husband who is engaged to a sweetheart who has everything would do well to take yet another look and see if she has money management sense." ("One for the Money," *Ensign,* July 1975, p. 72.)

Controlling your financial circumstances is another one of those "marriage skills" (and we put that in quotation marks) that obviously matters to everyone and matters long before entering into marriage. One of the great laws of heaven and earth is that your expenses need to be less than your income. You can reduce your anxiety and your pain and your early marital discord – indeed, you can reduce your *parents'* anxiety and pain and marital discord right now! – if you will learn to manage a budget.

JRH: As part of this general financial caution, we encourage, if necessary, plastic surgery for both husband and wife. This is a very painless operation, and it may give you more self-esteem than a new nose job or a tummy tuck. Just cut up your credit cards. Unless you are prepared to use those cards under the strictest of conditions and restraints, you should not use them at all – at least not at 18 percent or 21 percent or 24 percent interest. No convenience known to modern man has so jeopardized the financial stability of a family—especially young struggling families—as has the ubiquitous credit card. "Don't leave home without it?" That's precisely why he is leaving home—

PTH: —and why she is leaving him! May I paraphrase something President J. Reuben Clark said once in general conference:

"[Debt] never sleeps nor sickens nor dies; it never goes to the hospital; it works on Sundays and holidays; it never takes a vacation; . . . it is never laid off work . . . ; it buys no food; it wears no clothes; it is unhoused . . . ; it has neither weddings nor births nor deaths; it has no love, no sympathy; it is as hard and soulless as a granite cliff. Once in debt, [it] is your companion every minute of the day and night; you cannot shun it or slip away from it; you cannot dismiss it; . . . and whenever you get in its way or cross its course or fail to meet its demands, it crushes you." (*Conference Report,* April 1938, p. 103.)

JRH: Your religion should protect you against immorality and violence and any number of other family tragedies that strike at marriages throughout the land. And if you will let it, your religion will protect you against financial despair as well. Pay your tithes and offerings first. No greater financial protection can be offered you. Then simply budget what is left the rest of that month. Make do with what you have. Do without. Say no. Your head can be held high even if your clothing is not the most stylish or your home the most regal. It can be held high for the simple reason that it is not bent or bowed with the relentless burden of debt.

PTH: Well, that's more than we intended to say about money, but we remember how it was when we were just starting out.

JRH: I remember last month.

This last topic is the most difficult of all, and probably the most important. I hope we can communicate our feelings about it. Much has been said about the impropriety of intimacy before marriage. It is a message we hope you continue to hear often and one we hope you honor with the integrity expected of a Latter-day Saint man or woman. But now we wish to say something about intimacy *after* marriage, an intimacy that goes far beyond the physical relationship a married couple enjoy. Such an issue seems to us to be at the very heart of the true meaning of marriage.

PTH: Marriage is the highest and holiest and most sacred of human relationships. And because of that, it is the most intimate. When God brought Adam and Eve together before there was any death to separate them, he said, "Therefore shall a man leave his father and his mother, and shall cleave unto his wife: and they shall be one flesh." (Genesis 2:24.) To reinforce the imagery of that unity, the scriptures indicate that God had figuratively taken a rib from Adam's side to make Eve, not from his front that she should lead him and not from his back that she should despise him, but from his side, under his arm, close to his heart. There, bone of his bone and flesh of his flesh, husband and wife were to be united in every way, side by side. They were to give themselves totally to each other, and to "cleave unto [each other] and none else." (D&C 42:22.)

JRH: To give ourselves so totally to another person is the most trusting and perhaps the most fateful step we take in life. It seems such a risk and such an act of faith. None of us moving toward the altar would seem to have the confidence to reveal *everything* that we are—all our hopes, all our fears, all our dreams, all our weaknesses—to another person. Safety and good sense and this world's experience suggest that we hang back a little, that we not wear our heart on our sleeve where it can so easily be hurt by one who knows so much about us. We fear, as Zechariah prophesied of Christ, that we will be "wounded in the house of [our] friends." (Zechariah 13:6.)

But no marriage is really worth the name, at least not in

the sense that God expects us to be married, if we do not fully invest all that we have and all that we are in this other person who has been bound to us through the power of the holy priesthood. Only when we are willing to share life totally does God find us worthy to give life. Paul's analogy for this complete commitment was that of Christ and the church. Could Christ, even in his most vulnerable moments in Gethsemane or Calvary, hold back? In spite of what hurt might be in it, could he fail to give all that he was and all that he had for the salvation of his bride, his church, his followers— those who would take upon them his name even as in a marriage vow?

PTH: And by the same token, his church cannot be reluctant or apprehensive or doubtful in its commitment to him whose members we are. So, too, in a marriage. Christ and the church, the groom and the bride, the man and the woman must insist on the most complete union. Every mortal marriage is to recreate the ideal marriage sought by Adam and Eve, by Jehovah and the children of Israel. With no hanging back, "cleaving unto none other," each fragile human spirit is left naked, as it were, in the custody of its marriage partner, even as our first parents were in that beautiful garden setting. Surely that is a risk. Certainly it is an act of faith. But the risk is central to the meaning of the marriage, and the faith moves mountains and calms the turbulent sea.

JRH: It would be well worth our time if we could impress upon you the sacred obligation a husband and wife have to each other when the fragility and vulnerability and delicacy of the partner's life is placed in the other's keeping. Pat and I have lived together for twenty-two years—roughly the time that each of us had lived alone prior to the wedding day. I may not know everything about her, but I know twenty-two years' worth, and she knows that much of me. I know her likes and dislikes, and she knows mine. I know her tastes and interests and hopes and dreams, and she knows mine. As our love has grown and our relationship matured, we have been increasingly open with each other about all of that for twenty-two years now, and the result is that I know much more clearly how to help her and I know exactly how to hurt her. I may not know all the buttons to push, but I know most of them. And surely God will hold me accountable for any pain I cause her by intentionally pushing the hurtful ones when she has been so trusting of me. To toy with such a sacred trust—her body, her spirit, and her eternal future—and exploit those for my gain, even if only emotional gain, should disqualify me to be her husband and ought to consign my miserable soul to hell. To be that selfish would mean that I am a legal, live-in roommate who shares her company, but not her husband in any Christian sense of that word. I have not been as Christ is to the church. We would not be bone of one bone, and flesh of one flesh.

PTH: God expects a marriage, not just a temple-sanctioned understanding or arrangement of live-in wage earner or housekeeper. Surely everyone within the sound of my voice understands the severe judgment that comes upon such casual commitments before marriage. I believe there is an even more severe judgment upon me *after* marriage if all I do is share Jeff's bed and his work and his money and, yes, even his children. It is not marriage unless we literally share each other, the good times and the bad, the sickness and the health, the life and the death. It is not marriage unless I am there for him whenever he needs me.

JRH: You can't be a good wife or a good husband or a good roommate or a good Christian just when you "feel well." A student once walked into the office of Dean LeBaron Russell Briggs at Harvard and said he hadn't done his assignment because he hadn't felt well. Looking the student piercingly in the eye, Dean Briggs said, "Mr. Smith, I think in time you may perhaps find that most of the work in the world is done by people who aren't feeling very well." (Quoted by Vaughn J. Featherstone, "Self-Deal," *New Era*, November 1977, p. 9.)

Of course some days are going to be more difficult than

others, but if you leave the escape hatch in the airplane open because you think even before takeoff you might want to bail out in midflight, then I can promise you it's going to be a pretty chilly trip less than fifteen minutes after the plane leaves the ground. Close the door, strap on those seat belts, and give it full throttle. That's the only way to make a marriage fly.

PTH: Is it any wonder that we dress in white and go to the house of the Lord and kneel before God's administrators to pledge ourselves to each other with a confession of Christ's atonement? How else can we bring the strength of Christ to this union? How else can we bring his patience and his peace and his preparation? And above all, how else can we bring his permanence, his staying power? We must be bonded so tightly that *nothing* will separate us from the love of this man or this woman.

JRH: In that regard we have the most reassuring of all final promises: *That power which binds us together in righteousness is greater than any force — any force — which might try to separate us.* That is the power of covenant theology and the power of priesthood ordinances. That is the power of the gospel of Jesus Christ.

PTH: May I share just one concluding experience that, although taken from our marriage, has application to you right now — young or old, married or single, new convert or long-time member.

Twenty-two years ago, Jeff and I, marriage certificate in hand, made our way to Brigham Young University. We put all that we owned in a secondhand Chevrolet and headed for Provo. We were not uneasy. We were not frightened. We were terrified. We were little hayseeds from St. George, Utah, and here we were in Provo — at Brigham Young University, where the world was to be our campus.

The housing people were very helpful in providing lists of apartments. The registration staff helped straighten out some transfer credits. The folks in the employment center suggested where we might work. We pieced together some furniture and found some friends. Then we splurged, left our new forty-five-dollar-a-month, two-room-and-a-shower apartment to have an evening meal in the Wilkinson Center cafeteria. We were impressed and exhilarated and still terrified.

JRH: I remember one of those beautiful summer evenings walking up from our apartment on Third North and First East to the brow of the hill where the Maeser Building so majestically stands. Pat and I were arm in arm and very much in love, but school had not started, and there seemed to be so very much at stake. We were nameless, faceless, meaningless little undergraduates seeking our place in the sun. And we were newly married, each trusting our future so totally to the other, yet hardly aware of that at the time. I remember standing about halfway between the Maeser Building and the President's Home and being suddenly overwhelmed with the challenge I felt—new family, new life, new education, no money and no confidence. I remember turning to Pat and holding her in the beauty of that August evening and fighting back the tears. I asked, "Do you think we can do it? Do you think we can compete with all these people in all these buildings who know so much more than we do and are so able? Do you think we've made a mistake?" Then I said, "Do you think we should withdraw and go home?"

As a brief tribute to her in what has been a very personal message anyway, I guess that was the first time I saw what I would see again and again and again in her—the love, the confidence, the staying power, the reassurance, the careful handling of my fears and the sensitive nurturing of my faith, especially faith in me. She—who must have been terrified herself, especially now, linked to me for life—set aside her own doubts, slammed shut the hatch on the airplane, and grabbed me by the safety belt. "Of course we can do it," she said. "Of course we're not going home." Then, standing there, almost literally in the evening shadows of a home we would much later, for a time, call our own, she gently reminded me that surely others were feeling the same thing, that what we had in our hearts was enough to get us through, that our Father in heaven would be helping.

PTH: If you stand on the south patio of the President's Home, you can see the spot where two vulnerable, frightened, newly married BYU students stood twenty-two years ago, fighting back the tears and facing the future with all the faith they could summon. Some nights we stand and look out on that spot—usually nights when things have been a little challenging—and we remember those very special days.

Please don't feel you are the only ones who have ever been fearful or vulnerable or alone—before marriage or after. Everyone has, and from time to time perhaps everyone will yet be. Help each other. You don't have to be married to do that. Just be a friend, be a Latter-day Saint. And if you are married, no greater blessings can come to your union than some of the troubles and challenges you will face if you'll rev up your motor and bear straight ahead through lightning and thunder and turbulence and all.

JRH: Paraphrasing James Thurber in one of the best and simplest definitions of love ever given, "Love is what you go through together." That counts not only for husbands and wives but also parents and children, brothers and sisters, roommates and friends, missionary companions, and every other human relationship worth enjoying.

Love, like individuals, is tested by the flame of adversity. If we are faithful and determined, it will temper and refine us, but it will not consume us. Enjoy what you now have. Be a disciple of Christ. Live worthy of marriage even if it doesn't come soon. And cherish it with all your heart when it does.

ASSURANCES
AND AFFIRMATIONS

by Jeffrey R. Holland

Chapter 10

LIFT UP YOUR EYES

As Jesus walked and talked with the ordinary people of Galilee and Judea, there was nothing ordinary about his impact upon them. Although he taught them with a common touch, he elevated their lives in such remarkable ways that his must more properly be called an uncommon touch. While on the earth, he urged the grasp of very heavenly things.

Jesus gave us a living list of virtues through the example of his daily experience. One of those virtues that is especially needed in our routine contact with others—with family, friends, members, and nonmembers—is the rare ability to accept people for what they are, while lifting them toward what they can become. Whether dealing with devoted disciples close at hand or with publicans and prostitutes less familiar with such love, Jesus saw all of them as children of God. Some, he knew, were doing better than others, but all were in need of the higher, heavenly view he came to bring.

In his mingling with men and women of every background and station, Jesus demonstrated what could be called the common touch. His parables were directed toward the ordinary—toward fishermen and farmers, husbands and wives, servants and shepherds. And he was particularly conscious of the needy, the hungry stranger, and the imprisoned debtor—those whom others might consider the least among them. (See Matthew 25:35-40.)

115

Yet even as he walked and talked with the ordinary people of Galilee and Judea, there was nothing ordinary about his impact upon them. Although he taught them with a common touch, he elevated their lives in such remarkable ways that his must more properly be called an *un*common touch. There are many examples of his compassion linked with strong counsel, and of his patience coupled to urgent persuasion. Consider these few from the Gospel according to John.

Nicodemus was not so common in contemporary Judaic society. But he was one who nevertheless needed his vision enlarged and his life lifted. His need for the Master's touch revealed how universal that need was. In the sight of God, all needed the "new testament" written in their hearts regardless of social standing or ecclesiastical significance under the law of Moses. (See Jeremiah 31:33.)

John describes Nicodemus as "a man of the Pharisees, . . . a ruler of the Jews," a member of the powerful Jewish Sanhedrin. But in his groping toward the light, Nicodemus was, in a sense, as plain as all others darkened by apostasy and damaged by life lived without revelation. He was obviously haunted by what he heard and saw and felt coming from Jesus. On the other hand, he was not quite confident enough to come by day, publicly, and acknowledge Jesus' messiahship. His first remark seems tentative, almost exploratory. "We know that thou art a teacher come from God," he said, but in the record we have, he stops short of admitting the Savior's messiahship and shies away from asking what he must do to be saved.

Fortunately—as with others coming with other kinds of limitations—Jesus reached out to Nicodemus, inviting him to reach up: "Verily, verily, I say unto thee, Except a man be born again [or 'from above'], he cannot see the kingdom of God."

Nicodemus's response was confused. Conditioned by his Pharisaic literalism, he was either unwilling or unable to grasp the Savior's meaning and chose to give the reference to birth its most immediate meaning.

"How can a man be born when he is old? can he enter the second time into his mother's womb, and be born?" he asked.

Jesus patiently clarified: "Verily, verily, I say unto thee, Except a man be born of water and of the Spirit, he cannot enter into the kingdom of God."

Nicodemus must have looked either bewildered or incredulous, because Jesus continued, bringing down to the rabbi's level a teaching that apparently was too lofty for him to grasp otherwise. Master teacher that he was, Jesus seized on a double meaning of a Hebrew word and used it to lead Nicodemus from the temporal to the spiritual. In Hebrew the word *spirit* was rendered *ruah*, which also meant *puff* or *gust*, as a gust of wind. So, striving to teach of the Spirit, Jesus used the very word.

"Marvel not that I said unto thee, Ye must be born again. The wind bloweth where it listeth, and thou hearest the sound thereof, but canst not tell whence it cometh, and whither it goeth: so is every one that is born of the Spirit."

But Nicodemus seemed more confused than ever. "How can these things be?" he asked.

Jesus answered, "Art thou a master of Israel, and knowest not these things? . . . If I have told you earthly things, and ye believe not, how shall ye believe, if I tell you of heavenly things?" (John 3:1-12.)

Indeed, how can anyone understand spiritual, eternal truths if he is muddled about physical, temporal facts? If he does not understand the whispering source of the spirit, perhaps he will understand the whispering source of the wind as an earthly application of an otherwise heavenly teaching. We must come to understand heavenly things by starting where we are.

This same lesson is repeated — twice — in the next chapter of John's account. The geography, circumstances, and par-

117

ticipants are different, but obviously a common need runs through the fabric of Judaic life. It is clear that all people will need the Savior's uncommon touch if the scales of darkness are to fall from their eyes.

While traveling through Samaria among people intensely despised by the Jews of that day, Jesus and his disciples passed by the city of Sychar, "near to the parcel of ground that Jacob gave to his son Joseph." This area, which included within its borders Jacob's well, was uniquely symbolic of the Jewish-Samaritan animosity. Samaritans spoke strongly for their ancestral tie to Jacob—and the Jews denied them that assertion with equal vehemence. Did Jesus choose just such a location to lift the sight of both groups, too long limited by dark traditions?

While his disciples went into the city to buy food (it was the noon hour), Jesus sat on the stone perimeter of the well and watched a Samaritan woman approach with a waterpot in hand. The woman must have been very surprised to hear this Jewish traveler speak to her as she was preparing to lower her waterpot for water. Not only was a man speaking to a woman he did not know, but more strikingly, he was a Jew addressing a Samaritan. Nevertheless he said to her, "Give me to drink."

She questioned his request, as well she might, and Jesus had exactly the teaching situation he wanted. "If thou knewest the gift of God," he said, "and who it is that saith to thee, Give me to drink; thou wouldest have asked of him, and he would have given thee living water."

Here the Savior instantly introduced a hint of his true identity, a revelation that could indeed be "living water" to this woman if she could grasp heavenly things. But she showed no such inclination, wondering aloud how this man could possibly give her any water, living or otherwise, when he had nothing to draw with from such a deep well. Like Nicodemus, she struggled here even to understand earthly things.

Jesus went on. Referring to temporal sustenance, he said, "Whosoever drinketh of this water shall thirst again." Then he added, "But whosoever drinketh of the water that I shall give him shall never thirst; but the water that I shall give him shall be in him a well of water springing up into everlasting life."

This profound declaration so movingly spoken clearly captured the Samaritan woman's attention. But she was still caught up in the common, rather than the uncommon, possibilities. She could not see his higher purpose, but she was certainly interested in a perpetual source of water that would spare her these difficult daily trips to the well. "Sir," she said respectfully, "give me this water, that I thirst not, neither come hither to draw."

Jesus reached out one more time to help her understand. He tried to help by speaking of her most personal earthly things and asked her to call her husband. She replied that she had no husband. Jesus said, in effect, you certainly do not, and I include in that denial not only the man with whom you are now living but perhaps also the five who preceded him.

At this stunning revelation the woman cried out, "Sir, I perceive that thou art a prophet."

Surely it is fair to assume that Christ would have preferred to talk to the woman about living water rather than bogus husbands. But with her, as with Nicodemus, he met the student where she was in order to take her where she needed to go. Indeed, he took the most common of women in one of the most common, yet serious, sins and lifted her to uncommon opportunity. In response to her confession, "I know that Messias cometh, which is called Christ," he replied powerfully and pointedly: "I that speak unto thee am he." (John 4:25-26.)

Jesus seized on earthly things the woman could understand in order to lift her toward heavenly things she did not understand.

But what of others closer to Christ and stronger of spirit? We might suppose that a tradition-bound member of the Sanhedrin and an unfaithful woman of Samaria might have considerable difficulty breaking away from the commonplace which held them down. But what of Jesus' disciples? An answer to that question, at least in part, follows immediately in John's narrative.

Just as Jesus was concluding his discussion with the Samaritan woman, his disciples returned from the village with food for a midday meal, saying, "Master, eat. But he said unto them, I have meat to eat that ye know not of."

Obviously Jesus was referring to the "sustenance" of the experience he had just had with the Samaritan woman. He had, in a very few moments, lifted her from probable hostility and spiritual stupor to a state where she at least began to glimpse spiritual matters and heard in a wonderfully rare moment the Son of God declare himself to be the long-awaited Messiah. This was "meat" to one who fed on things of the Spirit—more so than a common crust of bread or literal cut of lamb so faithfully obtained in town by his brethren.

But very much like Nicodemus and the Samaritan woman before them, the disciples had not yet had enough experience to understand.

"Hath any man brought him ought to eat?" they asked in bewilderment. If he has had meat to eat we know not of, who brought it to him and why did he send us into the city? they wondered. Why would he have us make such an effort and then eat here with another before we return?

We smile slightly at this moment of confusion because we know what has transpired in the disciples' absence. Perhaps if they had known why Jesus was speaking to the woman and what he said, they would have more readily understood his reference to eating meat of quite a different kind. Christ's "meat," like his "living water," would leave one filled for eternity. In his gentle, patient, uncommon way, Christ lifted his beloved followers from the commonplace.

"My meat is to do the will of him that sent me, and to finish his work. Say not ye, There are yet four months, and then cometh harvest? Behold, I say unto you, Lift up your eyes, and look on the fields; for they are white already to harvest." (John 4:27-35.)

Jesus had seen an opportunity with eternal significance, and he seized it. For him, the field was *always* ready to harvest. He saw past the traditions and the wrangling and the pettiness of men. Indeed, he had even seen past the woman's very serious sins. What he saw was a chance to lift a life, to teach a human soul, to edify a child of God and move her toward salvation. That was his "meat" and his "work." Certainly it was the will of his Father that he had come to fulfill. Even these disciples who had become so close to the Master had yet to shed fully the scales of traditional darkness from their view. They, too, needed the uncommon invitation commonly extended to lift up their eyes to higher purposes, loftier meanings, more spiritual sustenance.

After noting a few such incidents, it becomes clear that this same lesson is taught by the Savior again and again. Jesus spoke of Temples and the people thought he spoke of temples. (John 2:18-21.) He spoke of Bread and the people thought he spoke of bread. (John 6:30-58.) And so on. And these were not merely parables in the allegorical sense of multiple applications of a single saying. They were in every case an invitation to "lift up your eyes," to see "heavenly things" — specifically to see and understand him. But they were also repeated manifestations of his willingness to meet people on their own terms, however limited that understanding, and there lead them on to higher ground. Ultimately, if they would, it would lead them beyond time and space altogether, into eternity.

As a reminder of the obligation for us to do likewise, consider this final application.

Following Jesus' crucifixion and resurrection, the plight and disarray of the disciples were perhaps best phrased by

121

Peter's declaration, "I go a fishing." Thinking perhaps their gospel task was concluded with the mortal conclusion of Christ's life, the other disciples said, "We also go with thee." In short, they went back to earthly endeavors.

But after a night's unsuccessful work with the nets, the disciples saw morning break and Jesus standing on the shore. After they returned to shore to be with him, he lifted them with his uncommon touch yet one more time.

To Simon Peter, chief apostle and he to whom the mantle of the mortal ministry and leadership had been passed, Jesus said: "Simon, son of Jonas, lovest thou me more than these?" Peter quickly reassured his Master, "Yea, Lord; thou knowest that I love thee."

Again a second time Jesus asked, "Simon, son of Jonas, lovest thou me?" Peter, now more troubled, reaffirmed anxiously, "Yea, Lord; thou knowest that I love thee."

Still a third time the Savior asked, "Simon, son of Jonas, lovest thou me?" and Peter, now openly aggrieved that the Savior would doubt him so, replied, "Lord, thou knowest all things; thou knowest that I love thee." (John 21:3-17.)

Perhaps it is both unnecessary and unfair to probe too deeply into this exchange. The great commandment given to Peter and the disciples here was to feed Christ's sheep, the little flock of followers who had already accepted him plus the multitude beyond their immediate circle who yet had need to hear and accept the gospel message. Clearly Peter was to be a fisher of men for the rest of his life and would need to forsake his nets at Galilee. Perhaps that is all that needs to be read here.

Furthermore, it may be sufficient to note that the thrice-repeated query and response could simply have served to reinforce the great significance of this task. Peter may have been particularly pained at *three* reminders after having denied association with the Savior thrice (see Matthew 26:34), but we have no reason to doubt the genuineness of his declared love. However, the New Testament language employed here does give one more powerful invitation to move from the commonplace of earthly things to the uncommon possibilities of heavenly things.

Although Jesus and Peter were not speaking Greek (they would have been speaking Aramaic), the account we have of John's Gospel record comes to us in that language. Two different Greek words for love are used in the exchange. In both the first and second inquiries, Jesus' question of Peter's love is asked in terms of *agape*, the highest form of love—what we would call Christlike or sacrificial love. But in reply, Peter's reassurance of love is rendered both times a different, lesser word—*philos*, or something more like brotherly love. Then it seems significant that in this third inquiry, Jesus himself uses the equivalent of *philos*, not *agape*, and Peter for the third time replies with *philos*.

It seems most appropriate that one of the great reminders in this final chapter of John's account is that Christ loves us where we are, even if that is not yet where we ought to be. Peter's brotherly love was acceptable, even though Jesus took this very setting to prophesy how much sacrificial, Christlike love Peter would soon be called upon to display and how magnificently he would do so. (See John 21:18-19.)

But that achievement for Peter—like Nicodemus, the Samaritan woman, and the other disciples—would come another day. What he and they could do was start now, where they stood, with what they had, common as it was. And through the miraculous touch of the Master's hand, they could be led to uncommonly exalted moments.

Wherever we are, we too can be on the way to heavenly things if we seek and accept the Savior's patient, ennobling *un*common touch.

Chapter 11

THE WILL
OF THE FATHER
IN ALL THINGS

*The work of devils and of darkness is never more certain
of defeat than when men and women, not finding it easy
or pleasant but still determined to do the Father's will,
look out upon their lives from which it may sometimes
seem every trace of divine help has vanished, and, asking
why they have been so forsaken, still bow their heads
and obey.*

Let me take a moment to set the stage for this chapter. I use the word *stage* advisedly. I want to suggest divine drama. Ralph Waldo Emerson once wrote, "If the stars should appear one night in a thousand years, how would men believe and adore; and preserve for many generations the remembrance of the city of God which had been shown [them]!" (*Nature* [1836], section 1.)

In the spirit of that very provocative thought, I invite you to consider another startling—and much more important—scene which should evoke belief and adoration, a scene which, like the stars at night, we have undoubtedly taken too much for granted. Imagine yourselves to be among the people of Nephi living in the land of Bountiful in approximately A.D. 34. Tempests and earthquakes and whirlwinds and storms, quickened and cut by thunder and sharp lightning, have enveloped the entire face of the land. Some cities—entire cities—have burst into flame as if by spontaneous combustion. Others have disappeared into the sea, never to be seen again. Still others are completely covered over with mounds of soil, and some have been carried away with the wind.

The whole face of the land has been changed; the entire earth around you has been deformed. Then, as you and your neighbors are milling about the temple grounds (a place that has suddenly seemed to many like a very good place to be), you hear a voice and see a man, clothed in a white robe, descending out of heaven. It is a dazzling display. He seems to emanate the very essence of light and life itself, a splendor in sharp contrast to the three days of death and darkness just witnessed.

He speaks and says simply, with a voice that penetrates the very marrow of your bones, "I am Jesus Christ, whom the prophets testified shall come into the world." (3 Nephi 11:10.)

There it is—or, more correctly speaking, there *he* is. The focal point and principal figure behind every fireside and devotional and family home evening held by those Nephites for the last six hundred years, and by their Israelite forefathers for thousands of years before that.

Everyone has talked of him and sung of him and dreamed of him and prayed—but here he actually is. This is the day and yours is the generation. What a moment! But you find you are less inclined to check the film in your camera than you are to check the faith in your heart.

"I am Jesus Christ, whom the prophets testified shall come into the world." Of all the messages that could come from the scroll of eternity, what has he brought to us? Everyone listens.

He speaks: "I am the light and the life of the world; . . . I have drunk out of that bitter cup which the Father hath given me, and have glorified the Father in taking upon me the sins of the world; . . . I have suffered the will of the Father in all things from the beginning." That is it. Eight lines. Fifty-two words." And . . . when Jesus had spoken these words the whole multitude fell to the earth." (3 Nephi 11:11-12.)

I have thought often about this moment in Nephite history, and I cannot think it either accident or mere whimsy that the Good Shepherd in his newly exalted state, appearing to a most significant segment of his flock, chooses to speak first of his obedience, his deference, his loyalty, and loving submission to his Father. In an initial and profound moment of spellbinding wonder, when surely he has the attention of every man, woman, and child as far as the eye can see, his submission to his Father is the first and most important thing he wishes us to know about himself.

Frankly, I am a bit haunted by the thought that this is the first and most important thing he may want to know about *us* when we meet him one day in similar fashion. Did we obey, even if it was painful? Did we submit, even if the cup was bitter indeed? Did we yield to a vision higher and holier than our own, even when we may have seen no vision in it at all?

One by one he invites us to feel the wounds in his hands and his feet and his side. And as we pass and touch and wonder, perhaps he whispers, "If any man will come after me, let him deny himself, and take up his cross, and follow me." (Matthew 16:24.)

If such cross-bearing self-denial was, by definition, the most difficult thing Christ or any man has ever had to do, an act of submission that would by the Savior's own account cause him, "God, the greatest of all, to tremble because of pain, and to bleed at every pore, and to suffer both body and spirit"—if yielding and obeying and bowing to divine will holds only that ahead, then no wonder that even the Only Begotten Son of the true and living God "would that [he] might not drink the bitter cup, and shrink"! (D&C 19:18.)

Even as we rehearse this greatest of all personal sacrifices, you can be certain that with some in this world it is not fashionable or flattering to speak of submitting to anybody or anything. At the threshold of the twenty-first century it sounds wrong on the face of it. It sounds feeble and wimpish. It just isn't the American way.

As Elder Neal A. Maxwell wrote recently, "In today's society, at the mere mention of the words *obedience* and *submissiveness*, hackles rise and people are put on nervous alert. . . . People promptly furnish examples from secular history to illustrate how obedience to unwise authority and servility to bad leaders have caused much human misery and suffering. It is difficult, therefore, to get a hearing for what the words *obedience* and *submissiveness* really mean—even when the clarifying phrase, 'to God', is attached." (*Not My Will, But Thine* [Salt Lake City: Bookcraft, 1988], p. 1.)

After all, we come to earth, at least in part, to cultivate self-reliance, to cultivate independence, to learn to think and act for ourselves. Didn't Christ himself say, "Ye shall know the truth, and the truth shall make you free"? (John 8:32.) So how does heaven speak of such spiritual freedom and intellectual independence in one breath, only to plead with us to be submissive and very dependent in the next?

It does so because no amount of education, or any other kind of desirable and civilizing experience in this world, will help us at the moment of our confrontation with Christ if we have not been able—and are not then able—to yield all that we are, all that we have, and all that we ever hope to have to the Father and the Son.

The path to a complete Christian experience most likely will pass through the Garden of Gethsemane. We will learn there, if we haven't learned it before, that our Father will have no other gods before him—even (or especially) if that would-be god is ourself. It will be required of each of us to kneel when we may not want to kneel, to bow when we may not want to bow, to confess when we may not want to confess— perhaps a confession borne of painful experience that God's thoughts are not our thoughts, neither are his ways our ways, saith the Lord. (See Isaiah 55:8.)

I believe that is why Jacob says to be learned—or, we

127

would presume, to be any other worthy thing—is good *if* one hearkens unto the counsels of God. (See 2 Nephi 9:29.) But education, or public service, or social responsibility or professional accomplishment of any kind is in vain if we cannot, in those crucial moments of pivotal personal history, submit ourselves to God even when all our hopes and fears may tempt us otherwise. We must be willing to place *all* that we have—not just our possessions (they may be the easiest things of all to give up) but also our ambition and pride and stubbornness and vanity—on the altar of God, kneel there in silent submission, and willingly walk away.

I believe that what I am describing here is the scriptural definition of a saint, one who "yields to the enticings of the Holy Spirit," and, "through the atonement of Christ, . . . becometh as a child, submissive, meek, humble, patient, full of love, willing to submit to all things which the Lord seeth fit to inflict upon him, even as a child doth submit to his father." (Mosiah 3:19.)

As the Great Exemplar and Daystar of our lives, is it any wonder that Christ chooses first and foremost to define himself in relation to his Father—that he loved him and obeyed him and submitted to him like the loyal son he was? And what he as a child of God did, we must try very hard to do also.

Obedience is the first law of heaven. And, in case we haven't noticed, some of these commandments are not easy. We frequently may seem to be in for much more than we bargained for. At least if we are truly serious about becoming saints, I think we will find that is the case. Let me use an example from what is often considered by foes, and even some friends, as the most unsavory moment in the entire Book of Mormon. I choose it precisely because there is so much in it that has given offense to many. It is pretty much a bitter cup all the way around.

I speak of Nephi's obligation to slay Laban in order to preserve a record, save a people, and ultimately lead to the restoration of the gospel in the dispensation of the fulness of times. How much is hanging in the balance as Nephi stands over the drunken and adversarial Laban I cannot say, but it is a great deal indeed. The dramatic irony here is that *we* know what a pivotal moment this is, but Nephi may not. And regardless of how much is at stake, how can he do this thing? He is a good person, perhaps even a well-educated person. He has been taught from the very summit of Sinai, "Thou shalt not kill." And he has made gospel covenants.

"I was constrained by the Spirit that I should kill Laban; but . . . I shrunk and would that I might not slay him." (1 Nephi 4:10.) A bitter test? A desire to shrink? Sound familiar? We don't know why those plates could not have been obtained some other way — perhaps accidently left at the plate polishers one night, or maybe falling off the back of Laban's chariot on a Sabbath afternoon drive. For that matter, why didn't Nephi just leave this story out of the book altogether? Why didn't he say something like, "And after much effort and anguish of spirit, I did obtain the plates of Laban and did depart into the wilderness unto the tent of my father"? At the very least he might have buried the account somewhere in the Isaiah chapters, thus guaranteeing that it would have gone undiscovered up to this very day.

But there it is, squarely in the beginning of the book, page eight, where even the most casual reader will see it — and must deal with it. It is not intended that either Nephi or we be spared the struggle of this account.

I believe that story was placed in the very opening verses of a 531-page book and then told in painfully specific detail in order to focus every reader of that record on the absolutely fundamental gospel issue of obedience and submission to the communicated will of the Lord. If Nephi cannot yield to this terribly painful command, if he cannot bring himself to obey, then it is entirely probable that he can never succeed or survive in the tasks that lie just ahead.

"I will go and do the things which the Lord hath commanded." (1 Nephi 3:7.) I confess that I wince a little when I hear that promise quoted so casually among us. Jesus knew what that kind of commitment would entail and so now does Nephi. And so will a host of others before it is over. That vow took Christ to the cross on Calvary and it remains at the heart of every Christian covenant. "I will go and do the things which the Lord hath commanded"? Well, we shall see.

In all of this we are, of course, probing Lucifer's problem, he of the raging ego, he who always took the Burger King motto too far and had to have everything his way. Satan would have done well to listen to that wisest of Scottish pastors who warned: "There is one kind of religion in which the more devoted a man is, the fewer proselytes he makes: the worship of himself." (C. S. Lewis, ed., *George MacDonald: An Anthology* [New York: Macmillan, 1947], p. 110.)

But Satan's performance can be instructive. The moment you have a self, there is the temptation to put it forward, to put it first and at the center of things. And the more we are — socially or intellectually or politically or economically — the greater the risk of increasing self-worship. Perhaps that is why when a newborn baby was brought before the venerable Robert E. Lee, the hopeful parents asked for this legendary man's advice, saying, "What should we teach this child? How should he make his way in the world?" And the wise old general said, "Teach him to deny himself. Teach him to say no."

Often such an exercise in submission is as lonely as it is wrenching. Sometimes, in those moments when we seem to need the Lord the very most, we are left to obey seemingly unaided. The psalmist cries out on behalf of all of us in such times: "Why standest thou afar off, O Lord? why hidest thou thyself in times of trouble?" "Why art thou so far from helping me? . . . I cry in the daytime, but thou hearest not; and in the night season, [I] am not silent." "Hide not thy face far from me, [Lord], . . . leave me not, neither forsake me, O

God of my salvation." "Be not silent [un]to me." (Psalms 10:1; 22:1-2; 27:9; 28:1.)

The psalmist's plea rings most painfully of that ultimate anguish on Calvary, that cry which characterized the act of supreme submission: "My God, My God, why hast thou forsaken me?" (Matthew 27:46. See also Psalm 22:1.) And to a lesser degree we hear the supplication from Liberty Jail: "O God, where art thou? And where is the pavilion that covereth thy hiding place? How long shall thy hand be stayed . . . ? Yea, O Lord, how long?" (D&C 121:1-3.)

We know a good deal about the abuse that Joseph and his colleagues suffered at the hands of their jailers. Furthermore, we know of Joseph's submissive spirit at that time, choosing then of all moments to pen some of the most sublime language in holy writ, the appeal to maintain influence only by "persuasion, by long-suffering, by gentleness and meekness, and by love unfeigned." (D&C 121:41.) What a setting in which to speak so kindly! What a brutal context in which to bring out such compassion!

But part of the story we don't remember so well is that of fellow prisoner Sidney Rigdon. Sidney was actually released from jail some two months before the Prophet Joseph and the others, but Rigdon left muttering that the sufferings of Jesus Christ were foolish compared to his.

Now it would not behoove us in the security of our pleasant quarters to pass judgment on Brother Rigdon or anyone else who suffered these indignities in Missouri, but to say that Christ's atoning sacrifice, bearing the weight of all the sins of all mankind from Adam to the end of the world, was foolishness compared to Brother Rigdon's confinement in Liberty Jail smacks of that defiant and finally fatal arrogance we so often see in those who end up in spiritual trouble.

Professor Keith Perkins has written that this moment marks the turning point for ill in Sidney Rigdon's life. (See "Trials and Tribulations: The Refiner's Fire" in *The Capstone of Our Religion: Insights into the Doctrine and Covenants* [Salt

Lake City: Bookcraft, 1989], p. 147.) After this experience he was no longer the distinguished leader he truly had been in the early years of the dispensation. Soon Joseph Smith felt him to be no longer of use in the First Presidency, and after the Prophet's death, Rigdon plotted against the Twelve in an effort to gain unilateral control over the Church. In the end he died a petty and bitter man, one who had lost his faith, his testimony, his priesthood, and his promises.

Joseph, on the other hand, would endure and be exalted when it was over. No wonder the Lord told him early in his life, "Be patient in afflictions, for thou shalt have many; but endure them, for, lo, I am with thee, even unto the end of thy days." (D&C 24:8.)

"What are these which are arrayed in white robes?" asks John the Revelator in his mighty vision. The answer: "These are they which came out of great tribulation, and have washed their robes, and made them white in the blood of the Lamb." (Revelation 7:13-14.)

Sometimes it seems especially difficult to submit to great tribulation when we look around and see others seemingly much less obedient who triumph even as we weep. But time is measured only unto man, says Alma (see Alma 40:8), and God has a very good memory.

Elder Dean L. Larsen writes of a Sabbath-observing farmer who was troubled and dismayed to see his Sabbath-breaking neighbor bring in far better crops with a much higher, more profitable yield. But in such times of seeming injustice, we must remember that "God's accounts are not always settled in October." ("The Peaceable Things of the Kingdom," in *Hope* [Salt Lake City: Deseret Book, 1988], p. 200.)

Sometimes, too, we underestimate the Lord's willingness to hear our cry, to confirm our wish, to declare that our will is not contrary to his and that his help is there only for the asking. Note this example taken from Elder F. Burton Howard's biography of President Marion G. Romney. I quote Elder Howard generously in summarizing this story.

In 1967 Sister Ida Romney suffered a serious stroke. The doctors told then-Elder Romney that the damage from the hemorrhage was severe. They offered to keep her alive by artificial means but did not recommend it. The family braced for the worst. Brother Romney confided to those closest to him that in spite of his anguished, personal yearning for Ida's restored health and continued companionship, above all he wanted "the Lord's will to be done and to take what he needed to take without whimpering."

As the days wore on, Sister Romney became less responsive. She had, of course, been administered to, but Elder Romney was "reluctant to counsel the Lord about the matter." Because of his earlier unsuccessful experience of praying that he and Ida might have children, he knew that he could never ask in prayer for something that was not in harmony with the will of the Lord. He fasted that he might know how to show the Lord he had faith and would accept God's will in their lives. He wanted to make sure he had done all he could do. But she continued to fail.

One evening in a particularly depressed state, with Ida unable to speak or recognize him, Brother Romney went home and turned, as he always had, to the scriptures in an effort to commune with the Lord. He picked up the Book of Mormon and continued where he had left off the night before. He had been reading in Helaman about the prophet Nephi, who had been falsely accused and unfairly charged with sedition. Following a miraculous deliverance from his accusers, Nephi returned home pondering the things he had experienced. As he did so he heard a voice.

Although Marion Romney had read that story many times before, it now struck him this night as a personal revelation. The words of the scripture so touched his heart that for the first time in weeks he felt he had tangible peace. It seemed as if the Lord were speaking directly to him. The scripture read: "Blessed art thou, . . . for those things which thou hast done; . . . thou hast not . . . sought thine own life, but hast sought my will, and to keep my commandments. And now, because thou hast done this with such unwearyingness, behold, I will bless thee forever; and I will make thee mighty in word and in deed, in faith and in works; yea, even that all things shall be done unto thee according to thy word, for thou shalt not ask that which is contrary to my will." (Helaman 10:4-5.)

There was the answer. He had sought only to know and obey the will of the Lord, and the Lord had spoken. He fell to his knees and poured out his heart, and as he concluded his prayer with the phrase "Thy will be done," he either felt or actually heard a voice that said, "It is not contrary to my will that Ida be healed."

Brother Romney rose to his feet quickly. It was past two o'clock in the morning, but he knew what he must do. Quickly he put on his tie and coat, then went out into the night to visit Ida in the hospital. He arrived shortly before three o'clock. His wife's condition was unchanged. She did not stir as he placed his hands upon her pale forehead. With undeviating faith, he invoked the power of the priesthood in her behalf. He pronounced a simple blessing and then uttered the incredible promise that she would recover her health and her mental powers and would yet perform "a great mission" upon the earth.

Even though he did not doubt, Elder Romney was astonished to see Ida's eyes open as he concluded the blessing. Somewhat stunned by all that had happened, he sat down on the edge of the bed only to hear his wife's frail voice for the first time in months. She said, "For goodness' sake, Marion, what are you doing here?" He didn't know whether to laugh or to cry. He said, "Ida, how are you?" With that flash of humor so characteristic of both of them, she replied, "Compared to what, Marion? Compared to what?"

Ida Romney began her recovery from that very moment, soon left her hospital bed, and lived to see her husband sustained as a member of the First Presidency of the Church, "a great mission upon the earth" indeed. (F. Burton Howard, *Marion G. Romney: His Life and Faith* [Salt Lake City: Bookcraft, 1988], pp. 137-42.)

We must be careful not to miss the hand of the Lord when it is offered, when it is his desire to assist. My daughter, Mary, made this point in a conversation with me not long after she had returned from a semester of study in Jerusalem. She was speaking of the ironic tendency to fear and avoid the very source of our help and deliverance, to retreat from rather than go toward our safety. She recalled the account in Matthew, when a storm arose on the Sea of Galilee and the ship containing the disciples was "tossed with waves: for the wind was contrary." In the midst of this anxiety the disciples looked toward the shore and saw a being, a ghost, an apparition walking directly toward them. This only increased their panic, and they began to cry out in fear. But it was Christ walking on the water toward them. "Be of good cheer," he called out. "It is I; be not afraid." (Matthew 14:24-27.) He was coming to help in their moment of need, and they, misunderstanding, were fleeing.

"Th[is] miracle is rich in symbolism and suggestion," wrote Elder James E. Talmage. "By what law or principle the effect of gravitation was superseded, so that a human body could be supported upon the watery surface, man is unable to affirm. The phenomenon is a concrete demonstration of the great truth that faith is a principle of power, whereby natural forces may be conditioned and controlled. Into every adult human life come experiences like unto the battle of the storm-tossed voyagers with contrary winds and threatening seas; ofttimes the night of struggle and danger is far advanced before succor appears; and then, too frequently the saving aid is mistaken for a greater terror. As came unto Peter and his terrified companions in the midst of the turbulent waters, so comes to all who toil in faith, the voice of the Deliverer—'It is I; be not afraid.' " (*Jesus the Christ* [Salt Lake City: Deseret Book, 1983], pp. 313-14.)

With that image of Christ again appearing in grandeur before us, let me conclude this drama where I began. We are taught that each one of us will come face-to-face with Christ to be judged of him, just as the world itself will be judged at his dramatic Second Coming. I close with an adaptation of an account by C. S. Lewis entitled "The World's Last Night," which I have commandeered and changed for the purposes of my message. The metaphor and much of the language are Lewis's, but the application is my own. In *King Lear* (Act III, scene vii) there appears a man who is such a minor character that Shakespeare has not even given him a name: he is simply called "First Servant." All the characters around him—Regan, Cornwall, and Edmund—have fine, long-term plans. They think they know how the story is going to end, and they are quite wrong. The servant, however, has no such delusions. He has no notion how the play is going to go. But he understands the present scene. He sees an abomination (the blinding of old Gloucester) taking place. He will not stand for it. His sword is out and pointed at his master's breast in an instant. Then Regan stabs him dead from behind. That is his whole part: eight lines all told. But, Lewis says, if that were real life and not a play, that is the part it would be best to have acted.

The doctrine of the Second Coming teaches us that we do not and cannot know when Christ will come and when the world drama will end. He may appear and the curtain may be rung down at any moment, say, before you have finished reading this paragraph. This kind of not knowing seems to some people intolerably frustrating. So many things would be interrupted. Perhaps you were going to get married next month; perhaps you were to buy a home next year. Perhaps you were thinking of going on a mission or paying your tithing or denying yourself some indulgence. Surely no good and wise God would be so unreasonable as to cut all that short. Not *now*, of all moments.

But we think this way because we keep on assuming that

we know the play. And, in fact, we don't know much about it. We believe we are "on" in Act II, but we know almost nothing of how Act I went or how Act III will be. We are not even sure we know who the major and who the minor characters are. The author knows. The audience—to the extent there is an audience of angels filling the loge and the stalls—has an inkling. But we—never seeing the play from the outside, and meeting only the tiny minority of characters who are on stage in the same scenes as we, and largely ignorant of the future and very imperfectly informed about the past—cannot tell at what moment Christ will come and confront us. We will face him one day—of that we may be sure; but we waste our time in guessing when that will be. That this human drama has a meaning we may be sure, but most of it we cannot yet fully see. When it is over, we will be told much more than we now know. We are led to expect that the Author will have something to say to each of us on the part that each of us has played. Playing it well, then, is what matters most. To be able to say at the final curtain, "I have suffered the will of the Father in all things," is our only avenue to an ovation in the end. (See "The World's Last Night," in *Fern-Seed and Elephants and Other Essays on Christianity by C. S. Lewis*, ed. Walter Hooper [Great Britain: Fontana/Collins, 1975], pp. 76-77.)

The work of devils and of darkness is never more certain of defeat than when men and women, not finding it easy or pleasant, but still determined to do the Father's will, look out upon their lives from which it may sometimes seem every trace of divine help has vanished, and, asking why they have been so forsaken, still bow their heads and obey. (Paraphrased from C. S. Lewis, *The Screwtape Letters* [New York: Macmillan, 1961], p. 39.)

To obey God's will "in all things" and to the very end is the only certain path open to believers. It is the only way to see his kingdom come and to make life "on earth as it is in heaven."

Chapter 12

O LORD, KEEP
MY RUDDER TRUE

*One who is disloyal may not have intended malice. He
or she may even be convinced that a certain good is
accomplished by such actions. In these cases it is well to
be reminded that some kinds of betrayal have a way of
producing results far beyond our control. We may have
only wanted to see someone cut down to size, but we
may live to see that we inadvertently cut that person to
ribbons.*

An event on the Brigham Young University campus several years ago was covered thoroughly by the press. The date was November 16, 1985. BYU made history. Television covered it, the print media published it, and in the best Clint Eastwood fashion, it made national sportscaster Beano Cook's day. BYU booed its own quarterback.

One of America's truly distinguished philosophers, Josiah Royce, wrote, "Loyalty is for the loyal man not only a good, but for him the chief amongst all the moral goods of his life, because it furnishes . . . him a personal solution [to] the hardest of [all] human . . . problems, the problem: 'For what do I live?' " (*The Philosophy of Loyalty* [New York: Macmillan, 1908], p. 57.)

It is loyalty—loyalty to true principles and true people and honorable institutions and worthy ideals—that unifies our purpose in life and defines our morality. Where we have no such loyalties or convictions, no standards against which

138

to measure our acts and their consequences, we are unanchored and adrift, "driven with the wind and tossed," says the scripture (James 1:6), until some other storm or problem or appetite takes us another direction for an equally short and unstable period of time. The older I get, the more I believe Professor Royce must have been right. "For what do I live?" is, in a sense, the inquiry every LDS missionary invites his or her investigator to make. If there is honest consideration of that question, then eternal truth has a fighting chance to bless the children of God. And such matters of loyalty and honor are important at BYU, for "to make [young people] capable of honesty," said John Ruskin, "is the beginning of education." Samuel Johnson said it even better: "Integrity without knowledge is weak and useless, and knowledge without integrity is dangerous and dreadful."

There are a lot of reasons why that booing incident bothers me. First of all it bothers me that any BYU fan would boo anybody for any reason. If someone can explain to me the Christianity of that, I invite him to do so quickly. Obviously it bothers me that such an experience would be seared by Mr. Cook into the entire national memory as the most regrettable moment of the collegiate football season. It bothers me that we would do this to a fellow student, a neighbor, a friend, a convert to the Church in this case. Not to mention, of course, that he also led us to two of our greatest years in BYU football history, including two conference championships, two post-season bowl games, a victory in the famed Kick-Off Classic, one undefeated season, and a national championship.

It bothers me that a very small handful of individuals could cast a cloud over a very fine game (which, by the way, BYU went on to win against a team that would end up fifth in the nation), and also cast something of a cloud over the whole season and, at least for me, cast a bit of a cloud over BYU football itself. At the same time I am confident that this small handful of rabid fans on virtually every other day of the week are probably pretty decent folks who wouldn't think of speaking so shamefully to anyone's face but who somehow get caught up—or get caught down, as the case may be—in the fervor of a game and watch their boorish behavior increase in direct proportion to the anonymity of the crowd and their own safe distance from a blitzing linebacker. Someone once said that no individual snowflake ever felt any responsibility for an avalanche. Maybe that is true for football fans as well.

We should be the kind of person who stands loyally by the principles and people and institutions to which we have declared allegiance, and that probably have given us most of the blessings we enjoy. In that sense what I say here has very little to do with fans or football or Beano Cook, whoever he is. The booing of a fellow human being is probably soon forgotten (except perhaps by the booee), so we apologize to him and all others who have received unchristian treatment at our hands and move on to ask the larger question: If every person had exactly the same sense of loyalty I have, what kind of neighborhood, or church, or nation, or world would ours be?

How much pressure is too much pressure to remain true? How much disappointment is too much disappointment to stand firm? How far is too far to walk with a discouraged friend, or a struggling spouse, or a troubled child? When the opposition heats up and the going gets tough, how much of what we thought was important to us will we defend and how much, in that inevitable tug and pull of life, will we find it convenient to give away?

As with so many abstractions that need to be made concrete, our homes and families are very good settings for an initial application. Would we, for example, stand by a younger brother or an older sister in times of despair or pain? Would we defend to the death our parents if they really needed our help? Even if our prayers are embarrassingly skimpy, don't we at least pray for the members of our family? I assume that those questions are easy to answer, because we say something

140

like: "Well, I love them," or "I owe it to them," or "They would do the same thing for me."

Yet what we so often fail to remember is that we should feel that way about everyone, that "family" is the true Christian appellation for the entire human race. Have we made the Sunday greeting of "Brother Jones and Sister Brown" too common to remember why we say it? Has our hasty reference to "Father in heaven" grown stale and insignificant? Will we ever widen our circle of influence beyond that already claimed by the Pharisees, who even in their benighted state did not boo other Pharisees? "What reward have ye? . . . And if ye salute your brethren only, what do ye more than others? do not even the publicans so?" (Matthew 5:46-47.) In matters of loyalty we all have a long way yet to go.

The late Alvin R. Dyer faced something of this challenge when he was a bishop many years ago. A member of his ward said that smoking was the greatest enjoyment he got out of life. He told Bishop Dyer, "At night I set my alarm every hour on the hour and wake up to smoke a cigarette. Bishop, I love smoking just too much to give it up."

A few evenings later the man's doorbell rang at ten o'clock. There on the doorstep was Bishop Dyer.

"Well, bishop, what on earth are you doing here at this hour? I'm ready to go to bed."

"I know," said Bishop Dyer. "I want to see you set that alarm and watch you wake up and smoke."

"Good heavens, I can't do that in front of you," the man said.

"Oh, sure you can. Don't worry about me. I'll just sit in a corner somewhere and be very quiet."

The man invited him in, and they talked about everything Bishop Dyer could conjure up to hold the man's interest. "I pursued every idea and conversation I could think of to keep him speaking," he recalled. "I thought he was going to throw me out a number of times, but shortly after three o'clock in the morning, I said, 'Well, heavenly days! You've missed five alarms already. Please forgive me. I have ruined your evening's enjoyment. The night is such a disappointment now that you might as well just go to bed and forget the rest of the alarms this once.' "

Then note this comment: "At that moment [I] felt [in him] a sense of honor and a dignity. . . . He looked at me with a peculiar smile . . . and he said, 'All right, I will.' [And] he never touched another cigaret [for the rest of his life]." (See Alvin R. Dyer, *Conference Report*, April 5, 1965, p. 85.)

How would you describe Brother Dyer's loyalty? Was it loyalty to that inactive man, or loyalty to the members of his ward generally, or loyalty to his office as bishop, or loyalty to the Word of Wisdom, or loyalty to the principle of revelation, or loyalty to the Church, or loyalty to God, or—well, you get my point.

His Father in heaven asks Cain, "Where is Abel thy brother?" and Cain fires back, "I know not: Am I my brother's keeper?" (Genesis 4:9.) Maybe the answer to that question is—as Professor Chauncey Riddle once said to me—"No, Cain, you are not expected to be your brother's keeper. But you are expected to be your brother's brother."

Consider for a moment the kind of treachery Cain introduced into the world—the betrayal of family, friends, and fellow citizens. His legacy is a chilling one and his colleagues are legion. "Dante reserve[d] the innermost circle of hell for [this crowd,] for those who [turn against their own]. There he placed Judas, Brutus and Cassius—the most notorious of traitors—in the three mouths of Satan himself. Revealingly, the poet does not rely on the image of fire for his description of their plight. The souls of traitors are held fast in a lake of ice. Clearly, the worst of sins against [one's] brother [or sister] are those of the frozen heart. Those who are disloyal to others have chosen a life isolated and immobile, a life, in effect, hostile to life, for which the only adequate image is a sunless waste of ice." (William F. May, *A Catalogue of Sins* [New York: Holt, Rinehart and Winston, 1967], pp. 111-12.)

If we are not called upon to defend a member of the family quite so openly as Cain was, perhaps we will have opportunities to defend the Church.

After four years of missionary service in the Hawaiian Islands (begun at age fifteen, by the way), young Joseph F. Smith returned to the mainland and began making his way back to the Salt Lake Valley. But these were difficult times. Feelings toward the Latter-day Saints were running very high. The terrible experience at Mountain Meadows was fresh in the minds of many people. Polygamy had become a national political issue, and at that very hour Albert Sidney Johnston's army was on its way to the Utah territory under orders from the president of the United States. Less disciplined than the U. S. Army were many frontiersmen scattered abroad who vowed openly they would murder every Mormon anywhere they could be found.

It was back into that world that nineteen-year-old Joseph F. Smith drove his team and wagon. One evening the little company with which he traveled had barely made camp before a company of drunken men rode in on horseback, cursing and swearing and threatening to kill. Some of the older men, when they heard the riders coming, went down into the brush by the creek, waiting out of sight for the band to pass. But young Joseph F. had been out a distance from the camp gathering wood for the fire and so was not aware of the potential problem. With the openness of youth he walked back toward the camp, only to realize too late the difficult circumstance he now faced almost totally alone.

His first thought was to drop the wood and run toward the creek, seeking shelter in the trees in his flight. Then the thought came to him, "Why should I run from [my faith]?" With that compelling sense of loyalty firmly in his mind, he continued to carry his armful of wood to the edge of the fire. As he was about to deposit his load, one of the ruffians, pistol cocked and pointed squarely at the young man's head, cursed

143

as only a drunken rascal can and demanded in a loud, angry voice, "I'm a killer of Mormons, boy. Are you a Mormon?"

Without a moment of hesitation and looking the heathen directly in the eye, Joseph F., scarcely old enough to be entering the Missionary Training Center, boldly answered, "Yes, siree; died in the wool; true blue, through and through."

The answer was given so boldly and without any sign of fear that it completely disarmed this belligerent man. In his bewilderment he put down his pistol, grasped the young missionary by the hand, and said, "Well, you are the [blank] [blank] pleasantest man I ever met! Shake, young fellow, I am glad to see a man that stands up for his convictions."

Years later, while serving as the president of the Church, Joseph F. Smith said that he truly expected to take at point-blank range the full charge from the barrel of that man's pistol. But he also said that after his initial inclination to run, it never again entered his mind to do anything but stand up for his belief and face the death that appeared to be the inevitable result of such conviction. (Joseph Fielding Smith, *Life of Joseph F. Smith* [Salt Lake City: Deseret News Press, 1938], pp. 188-89.)

Montaigne's ancient cry of the storm-tossed sailor comes to mind: "O God! thou mayest save me if thou wilt, and if thou wilt, thou mayest destroy me: but whether or no, I will steer my rudder true." (Montaigne, *Essays*, book II, chapter 16.)

Of course, it is not enough to be loyal to just any cause. What carried nineteen-year-old Joseph F. Smith so courageously was his answer to the question: "For what do I live?" It was for gospel truth that he stood up to be counted and that he was willing to die.

Brigham Young certainly had repeated opportunities to hold a steady course, particularly in those early and difficult years at the side of the Prophet Joseph Smith. While the First Presidency was away from Kirtland attempting to stabilize the difficult financial circumstances they faced in the winter of 1836-37, a council was called by those opposed to Joseph Smith's continuing in his office as prophet and president of the Church.

"On this occasion [Brigham Young] rose up . . . in a plain and forcible manner and told them 'that Joseph was a Prophet, and I knew it, and that they might rail and slander him as much as they pleased; they could not destroy the appointment of the Prophet of God, they could only destroy their own authority, cut the thread that bound them to the Prophet and to God, and sink themselves to hell.' Some of those present reacted violently [toward Brigham]. Jacob Bump . . . fancied himself a pugilist. While several held him back, he twisted and turned, shouting, 'How can I keep my hands off that man?' 'Lay them on,' responded Brigham, 'if it will give you any relief.' "

But the man didn't lay them on. A few nights later Brigham heard a man running through the Kirtland streets at midnight, shouting loudly and denouncing the Prophet Joseph. Even at that late hour Brigham jumped out of bed, went into the street, "jerked [the man] round, and assured him that if he did not stop his noise, and let the people enjoy their sleep," he would "cowhide him on the spot, for we had the Lord's Prophet right here, and we did not want the devil's prophet yelling [up and down] the streets."

These were days of genuine crisis, he reported, "when earth and hell seemed leagued to overthrow the Prophet and the Church of God. The knees of many of the strongest men in the Church faltered." Brigham Young did not falter, yet before that year was over, his own life was in jeopardy for such loyalty. On December 22 he said, "I had to leave to save my life. . . . I left Kirtland in consequence of the fury of the mob, and the spirit that prevailed in the apostates, who had threatened to destroy me because I would proclaim, publicly and privately, that I knew by the power of the Holy Ghost, that Joseph Smith was a Prophet of the Most High God."

(Leonard J. Arrington, *Brigham Young, American Moses* [New York: Alfred A. Knopf, 1985], pp. 56-61.)

And what of Joseph Smith himself? Even as he was being dragged away from his wife and children one more time, he said, "I am exposed to far greater danger from traitors among ourselves than from enemies without. . . . All the enemies upon the face of the earth may roar and exert all their power to bring about my death, but they can accomplish nothing, unless some who are among us and enjoy our society . . . bring their united vengeance upon our heads." (*History of the Church* 6:152.)

And bring their united vengeance they did. Does a prophet of God deserve that from his "friends"? What does one have a right to expect from those who "enjoy our society"? (Remember that Macbeth's crime against his king was all the more treacherous because Duncan was a guest in Macbeth's house.) Is it possible that each of us who claim the privileges and benefits of the kingdom of God will have our own fiery furnace to pass through in which our loyalty is purified as dramatically as it was for Shadrach, Meshach, and Abed-nego? Is there some kind of battleground out there ahead of us, some kind of moral Kirtland or metaphysical Carthage that will give us our chance to stand up and be counted, like the two thousand stripling warriors of whom it was said, "They were . . . true at all times in whatsoever thing they were entrusted"? (Alma 53:20.)

Karl G. Maeser, the first president of Brigham Young University, once wrote, "I have been asked what I mean by the word honor. I will tell you. Place me behind prison walls — walls of stone ever so high, ever so thick, reaching ever so far into the ground — there is a possibility that in some way or another I may be able to escape; but stand me on the floor and draw a chalk line around me and have me give my word of honor never to cross it. Can I get out of that circle? No, never! I'd die first!"

From time to time we all ought to look deeply into our

souls and habits and inclinations and measure our loyalties against the divine standard of our Savior, Jesus Christ. How prepared are we for the difficult things we may yet face in acquiring an education or serving a mission or raising a family or defending our beliefs? As preparation for the assault that will yet be made upon our character and convictions, is it hoping too much to see us cherish clear language and clean entertainment and hard work and disciplined behavior? If we were, this very hour, in a fictional foxhole somewhere against an enemy who put our eternal lives at risk, would I be safe in your hands? Would you be safe in mine?

More than thirty years ago about fifteen LDS soldiers crowded into a frontline bunker in Korea to hold a Sunday service. They used their canteen cups and C-ration crackers to bless and partake of the sacrament. Then they held a testimony meeting. One young man introduced himself simply as Sergeant Stewart from Idaho. He was a short, small man about 5 feet 5 inches tall and weighing about 150 pounds. His great ambition had been to become a good athlete, but coaches considered him too small for most team sports. So he had concentrated on individual competition and had gained some success as a wrestler and a distance runner. Sergeant Stewart related to his fourteen battle-weary brethren an experience he had just had with his company commander, a giant of a man named Lieutenant Jackson, who was 6 feet 7 inches tall, weighed 245 pounds, and was an outstanding college athlete. The sergeant spoke of him in glowing terms as a tremendous officer and a Christian gentleman, inspiring those who were fortunate enough to serve under his command.

Shortly before the Church service in which they now found themselves, Sergeant Stewart had been assigned to a patrol under the direction of Lieutenant Jackson. As they moved down near the base of a hill they held, they were ambushed by enemy fire. The lieutenant out in front was "riddled . . . by automatic small-arms fire. As he fell he managed to drag himself to the shelter of a rock . . . while the

147

rest of the patrol scrambled up the hill to regroup. Since he was second in command, responsibility now fell upon Sergeant Stewart. He [sent the] largest and seemingly strongest man . . . down the hill to rescue the lieutenant. The others would provide him with cover.

"The man was gone for approximately half an hour, only to return and report that he could not budge the wounded officer—he was too heavy. . . . The men started grumbling about getting out of there before somebody else got hit. [Then] someone was heard to say, 'Let's forget about the lieutenant; after all, he's just a nigger!' At this point Sergeant Stewart turned to his men, and pulling himself up to his full 65-inch stature, he spoke in very matter-of-fact tones: 'I don't care if he's black or green or any other color. We're not leaving without him. He wouldn't leave any of us in similar circumstances. Besides, he's our commanding officer and I love him like my own brother.' "

Then he headed down the hill alone.

Sergeant Stewart finally reached the officer and found that he was weak from loss of blood. The lieutenant assured the sergeant that it was a hopeless cause—there would be no way to get him back to the aid station in time. "It was then that Sergeant Stewart's great faith in his Heavenly Father came to his assistance. He took off his helmet, knelt beside his fallen leader, and said, 'Pray with me, Lieutenant.' . . .

" 'Dear Lord,' he pleaded, 'I need strength—far beyond the capacity of my physical body. This great man, thy son, who lies critically wounded here beside me, must have medical attention soon. I need the power to carry him up this hill to an aid station where he can receive the treatment he needs to preserve his life. I know, Father, that thou hast promised the strength of ten to him whose heart and hands are clean and pure. I feel that I can qualify. Please, Dear Lord, grant me this blessing.' "

He thanked his Father in heaven for the power of prayer and the privilege of holding the priesthood. Then he put on his helmet, reached down and picked up his fallen leader, cradled him over his shoulders, and carried him back up the hill to safety. (Ben F. Mortensen, "Sergeant Stewart," *The Instructor*, March 1969, pp. 82-83.)

Someone else ascended a difficult hill once – with us cradled carefully on his shoulders. But as Christ moved closer and closer to Calvary, his defenders became fewer and fewer in number. As the pressure mounted and the troubles increased, he said, "There are some of you that believe not. For Jesus knew from the beginning who they were that believed not, and who should betray him. . . . From that time many of his disciples went back, and walked no more with him." (John 6:64, 66.)

Later, when the Roman soldiers and the chief priests – "a great multitude with swords and staves," Matthew says – came to capture him, "all the disciples forsook him, and fled." (Matthew 26:47, 56.)

Enter Judas with the calculated kiss of betrayal.

We cannot know exactly what Judas was thinking nor why he chose the path he did. Perhaps he did not think it would end that way. As William F. May said, a person who is disloyal may not intend malice – "he may even be convinced that he accomplishes a certain good by his actions. In these cases, it is well to be reminded that [some kinds of] betrayal [have] a way of producing results beyond [our] . . . control. [A sequence] more savage than [we] intended. [I take a certain stand or make a certain speech toward another], only wanting to see him cut down to size, but I may live to see him cut into ribbons. . . .

"When Judas, [Jesus'] betrayer, saw that he was condemned, he repented and brought back the thirty pieces of silver to the chief priests and the elders, saying, 'I have sinned in betraying innocent blood.' They said, 'What is that to us? See to it yourself.' Precisely because everything has been placed beyond the traitor's reach . . . , the sense of the irreversibility of it all is overwhelming. There is nothing left to be done. Judas hangs himself, [perhaps] as an act of an atonement, . . . but [also perhaps] because no [act] of atonement—from Judas—is [any longer] possible." (William F. May, *A Catalogue of Sins*, pp. 118-19.)

Yet it is also here in this hour, in absolute and utter loneliness, that loyalty to principle and love for one's brothers and sisters reaches its most exalted and eternal manifestation. Sweating great drops of blood from every pore and pleading that the cup might pass, yet Jesus remains true, submitting his will to that of his Father and determined to do the work of the kingdom. Moments later, with taunts and spit and scorn and jeers, and spikes rending his perfect flesh, principle triumphs over both passion and pain as the Savior of us all prays for his brothers and sisters, "Father, forgive them; for they know not what they do." (Luke 23:34.)

We should give our deepest loyalties to the highest causes in eternity—those contained in the life and mission and gospel and teachings of the Only Begotten Son of God. If we can remain true there, with an eye single to that standard, all other loyalties will fall naturally into place. Consider these verses from two popular hymns. To all who wish to know heaven's determination to stand by them in difficult times, we sing:

> *The soul that on Jesus hath leaned for repose*
> *I will not, I cannot, desert to his foes;*
> *That soul, though all hell should endeavor to shake,*
> *I'll never, no never, no never forsake!*
> —*Hymns*, 1985, no. 85

And for the personal strength to stand true, even in such times of personal pain, we sing more privately to ourselves:

> *He has sounded forth the trumpet that shall never call retreat;*
> *He is sifting out the hearts of men before his judgment seat.*
> *Oh, be swift, my soul, to answer him; be jubilant, my feet!*
> *Our God is marching on.*
> —*Hymns*, 1985, no. 60

150

Chapter 13

THE BITTER CUP AND
THE BLOODY BAPTISM

*God wants us stronger than we are—more fixed in our
purpose, more certain of our commitments, eventually
needing less coddling from him, showing more willingness to shoulder some of the burden of his heavy load.
In short, he wants us to be more like him.*

I n the final few weeks of 1944 I was bundled up and taken,
at about six in the morning as I recall, down to the Big
Hand Cafe on the corner of Main Street and Highway
91 in St. George, Utah. That's where the Greyhound bus
stopped in our little town, and that morning my Uncle Herb,
all of seventeen years of age, was leaving for San Diego,
California—wherever that was. Apparently in 1944 there was
a war on somewhere, and he was now deemed old enough
to go and do his part. He had joined the United States Navy,
and we were there to say goodbye.

Actually, I had a rather formal part in this bus-stop program. I had practiced and was now supposed to sing in my
four-year-old solo voice a little ditty that celebrated sailors,
with lyrics beginning "Bell-bottom trousers / Coat of navy
blue. / She loves her sailor boy / And he loves her too." However, as with other assignments later in my life, I panicked
in the public eye and went stone silent. I refused to sing a
note.

But my silence seemed to work out all right anyway,
because my mother and my grandmother and my aunts were

all crying and nobody cared much whether I sang or not. I asked why they were crying, and they said it was because Uncle Herb was going to war. I asked, "How long will he be gone?"—not knowing then that some of the boys were never coming home. Through her tears my grandmother said, "He will be gone as long as it takes. He will be gone for the duration of the war."

Well, I had no idea whatsoever of her meaning. "As long as it takes to do what?" for crying out loud—which is exactly what they were doing. And what was "the duration of the war"? I was totally confused and very glad I didn't sing my song. That would only have added to the confusion, and the Big Hand Cafe never could stand much confusion.

I have thought a lot more about my grandmother's words later in my life than I ever thought about them in my youth. The longer I live, the more I come to realize that some things in life are very true and very permanent and very important. They are matters that might collectively be labeled eternal things. Without listing a whole catalog of these good and permanent possessions, it is sufficient to say that all of them are included collectively, in some way or another, in the gospel of Jesus Christ. As Mormon told his son, "In Christ there . . . come[s] every good thing." (Moroni 7:22.) So, as time goes by, we ought—as a matter of personal maturity and growth in the gospel—to spend more of our time with and devote more of our energy to the good things, the best things, the things that endure and bless and prevail.

This is why, I believe, family and true friends become increasingly important the older we get, and so does knowledge, and so do simple acts of kindness and concern for the circumstances of others. Peter lists a whole handful of these virtues, calling them "the divine nature," and he promises us "divine power" in possessing and sharing them. (See 2 Peter 1:3-8.) These gospel qualities and principles, as I understand them, are the most important as well as the most permanent of life's acquisitions. But there is a war going on

over such personal possessions, and there will yet be a ba-
zooka shell or two falling into our lives that will prompt—
indeed, will require—careful examination of what we say we
believe, what we assume we hold dear, and what we trust is
of permanent worth.

When difficult times come upon us or when temptation
seems all around, will we be—are we now?—prepared to
stand our ground and outlast the intruder? Are we equipped
for combat, to stay loyal for as long as it takes, to stay true
for the duration of the war? Can we hold fast to the principles
and the people who truly matter eternally to us?

In order for us to determine the quality of our faith, the
determination of our purpose, we must more clearly understand the commitment we made when we were baptized not
only into Christ's church, but into his life and his death and
his resurrection, into all that he is and stands for in time and
in eternity. We have made promises—to ourselves and to our
God. Those who have been endowed in the holy temple have
taken upon themselves the highest covenants and holiest ordinances available in mortality.

We are a people who have already thrust ourselves into
the most serious and most eternal of issues. The war is on,
and we have conspicuously enlisted. And certainly it is a war
worth waging. But we are foolish, fatally foolish, if we believe
it will be a casual or convenient thing. We are foolish if we
think it will demand nothing of us. Indeed, as the chief figure,
the great commander in this struggle, Christ has warned us
about treating the new testament of his body and his blood
trivially. We are told emphatically not to pilfer or profane,
prevaricate or fornicate, or satiate ourselves in every indulgence or violation that strikes our fancy, and then suppose
that we are still "pretty darn good soldiers." No, not in this
army, not in defending the kingdom of God.

More is expected than that. *Much* more is needed. And
in a very real sense, eternity hangs in the balance. I truly
believe there can be no casual Christians, for if we are not

watchful and resolute, we will become in the heat of battle a Christian "casualty." And each of us knows some of those. Perhaps we ourselves have at some time been wounded. We weren't strong enough. We hadn't cared enough. We didn't stop to think. The war was more dangerous than we had supposed. The temptation to transgress, to compromise, is all around us, and too many of us, even as members of the Church, have fallen victim. We have partaken of Christ's "flesh and blood unworthily," and we have eaten and drunk damnation to our souls. (3 Nephi 18:28-29.)

Some of us may *still* be taking such transgression lightly, but at least the Master understands the significance of the side we say we have chosen. His understanding was powerfully revealed in his teachings to the disciples.

At the conclusion of his Perean ministry, Jesus and the Twelve were making their way back to Jerusalem for that last, prophetically foretold week leading up to his arrest, trial, and crucifixion. In that most sober and foreboding sequence of events, the Savior — who singly and solitarily alone knew what lay ahead of him and just how difficult the commitments of his final hours would be — was approached by the mother of two of his chief disciples, James and John. She rather straightforwardly asked a favor of the Son of God: "Grant that these my two sons may sit, the one on thy right hand, and the other on the left, in thy kingdom." (Matthew 20:21.)

This good mother and perhaps most of the little band who had faithfully followed Jesus were obviously preoccupied by the dream and expectation of that time when this, their Messiah, would rule and reign in splendor — when, as the scripture says, "the kingdom of God should immediately appear." (Luke 19:11.)

The question the mother asked was more one of ignorance than impropriety, and Christ uttered not a word of rebuke. He gently answered as one who always considered the consequence of any commitment.

"Ye know not what ye ask," he said quietly. "Are ye able

to drink of the cup that I shall drink of?" This startling question did not take James and John by surprise. Promptly and firmly they replied, "We are able." And Jesus's response to them was, "Ye shall drink indeed of my cup, and be baptized with the baptism that I am baptized with." (Matthew 20:22-23.)

Without any reference to the glory or special privilege James and John seem to have been seeking, this may strike one as a strange favor the Lord was granting them. But he was not mocking them by offering the cup of his suffering rather than a throne in his kingdom. No, he had never been more serious. The cup and the throne were inextricably linked and could not be given separately.

I am sure that we Latter-day Saints, being not only less worthy than Christ but also less worthy than apostles like James and John, would leave such troublesome issues alone if they would only leave us alone. As a rule we usually do not seek the bitter cup and the bloody baptism, but sometimes they seek us. The fact of the matter is, God *does* draft men and women into the spiritual warfare of this world, and if any of us come to genuine religious faith and conviction as a result of that—as many a drafted soldier has done—it will nevertheless be a faith and a conviction that in the first flames of the battle we did not enjoy and certainly did not expect. (See A. B. Bruce, *The Training of the Twelve* [New York: Richard R. Smith, 1930].)

Let us put ourselves in the place of James and John, put ourselves in the place of seemingly committed, believing, faithful Latter-day Saints, and ask ourselves, "If we are Christ's and he is ours, are we willing to stand firm forever? Are we in this church for keeps, for the duration, until it's over? Are we in it through the bitter cup, the bloody baptism, and all?" I am not asking if any of us can simply endure our years as a young adult or serve out a term as gospel doctrine teacher. I am asking questions of a far deeper and more fundamental sort. I am asking about the purity of our hearts. How cherished are our covenants? Have we—perhaps beginning our life in the Church as a result of parental insistence or geographic happenstance—have we yet thought about a life that is ultimately to be tempted and tried and purified by fire? Have we cared about our convictions enough and are we regularly reinforcing them in a way that will help us do the right thing at the right time for the right reason, especially when it is unpopular or unprofitable or nearly unbearable to do so?

Indeed, we may one day be released as the glamorous gospel doctrine teacher and be called to that much vacated post of gospel doctrine believer and obeyer. That will test our strength! Surely our sometimes clichéd expressions of testimony and latter-day privilege do not amount to much until we have had open invitation to test them in the heat of battle and have in such spiritual combat found ourselves to be faithful. We may speak glibly in those Sunday services of *having* the truth or even of *knowing* the truth, but only one who is confronting error and conquering it, however painfully or however slowly, can properly speak of *loving* the truth. And I believe Christ intends us someday to truly, honestly *love* him—the way, the truth, and the life.

Tragically enough, the temptation to compromise standards or be less valiant before God often comes from another member of the Church. Elder William Grant Bangerter wrote of his experience years ago in the military shortly after he had returned from his mission. "I realize," he concluded, "that throughout those years I was considered different. . . . [But] I never found it necessary to break my standards, to remove my garments, or to apologize for being a Latter-day Saint." Then he made this very telling observation: "I can honestly say that no nonmember of the Church has ever tried to induce me to discard my [LDS] standards. The only people I remember trying to coerce me to abandon my principles or who ridiculed me for my standards have been non-practicing members of [my own] church." ("Don't Mind Being Square," *New Era*, July 1982, p. 6.)

Because we have been given so much, we must be prepared to stand by principle and act on conviction, even if that seems to leave us standing alone. Remember these lines from *Paradise Lost:*

> *I alone*
> *Seemed in thy world erroneous to dissent*
> *From all; my sect thou seest. Now learn too late*
> *How few sometimes may know, when thousands err.*
> *— Book VI, lines 145-48*

We work and live in a world where *many* people err — many more than Milton's thousands. But however difficult and lonely it may seem, we must not be numbered among those who err; we must live by the highest principles and stand firmly by our faith. We will undoubtedly be tempted, but we must be strong. The cup and the throne are inextricably linked.

Perhaps so far we have considered the rather obvious transgressions Latter-day Saints face, the temptations Satan never seems to keep very subtle. But what about the gospel-living that isn't so obvious and may be of a higher order still? Let us shift both the tone and the temptations just slightly, and cite other examples of our Christian challenge.

On the night of March 24, 1832, a dozen men stormed the Hiram, Ohio, home where Joseph and Emma Smith were staying. Both were physically and emotionally spent, not only from all the travails of the young church at the time but also because on this particular evening they had been up caring for their two adopted twins, born eleven months earlier on the same day that Emma had given birth to and then lost their own twins. Emma had gone to bed first while Joseph stayed up with the children; then she had arisen to take her turn, encouraging her husband to get some sleep. No sooner had he begun to doze than he heard his wife give a terrifying scream, and he found himself being torn from the house and very nearly being torn limb from limb.

157

Cursing as they went, the mobbers who had seized Joseph were swearing to kill him if he resisted. One man grabbed him by the throat until he lost consciousness from lack of breath. He came to only to overhear part of their counsel as to whether he should be murdered. It was determined that for now he would simply be stripped naked, beaten senseless, tarred and feathered, and left to fend for himself in the bitter March night.

Stripped of his clothing, fighting off fists and tar paddles on every side, and resisting a vial of some liquid, perhaps poison, which he shattered with his teeth as it was forced into his mouth, he miraculously managed to fight off the entire mob and eventually made his way back to the house. In the dim light his wife thought the tar stains covering his body were blood stains, and she fainted at the sight. Friends spent the entire night scraping and removing the tar and applying liniments to his scratched and battered body. I now quote directly from the Prophet Joseph's record:

"By morning I was ready to be clothed again. This being the Sabbath morning, the people assembled for meeting at the usual hour of worship, and among them came also the mobbers [of the night before, whom he then names]. With my flesh all scarified and defaced, I preached to the congregation as usual, and in the afternoon of the same day baptized three individuals." (*History of the Church* 1:264.)

Unfortunately, one of the adopted twins, growing worse from the exposure and turmoil of the night, died the following Friday. "With my flesh all scarified and defaced, I preached to the congregation as usual." Preached to that slimy band of cowards who by Friday next will quite literally be the murderers of your child? Stand there hurting from the hair of your head that was pulled and then tarred into a mat, right down to your foot, which was nearly torn off while being wrenched out the door of your own home? Preach the gospel to that damnable bunch of sniveling reprobates? Surely this is no time to stand by principle! It is daylight now, and the odds aren't twelve to one anymore. Let's just conclude this Sunday service right now and go outside to finish last evening's business. It was, after all, a fairly long night for Joseph and Emma; maybe it should be an appropriately short morning for this dirty dozen who have snickeringly shown up for church.

But those feelings that I have even now, just reading about this experience 150 years later—and feelings I know that would have raged in my Irish blood that morning—mark only one of the differences between me and the Prophet Joseph Smith. A disciple of Christ—which I testify Joseph was and is—always has to be a disciple; the judge does not give any time off for bad behavior. A Christian always stands on principle, even as I think of being out there swinging a pitchfork and screaming an eye for an eye and a tooth for a tooth, forgetting, as dispensation after dispensation has forgotten, that this only leaves everyone blind and toothless.

No, the good people, the strong people, dig down deeper and find a better way. Like Christ, they know that when it is hardest to be so is precisely the time you have to be at your best. I have always feared that *I* could not have said at Calvary's cross, "Father, forgive them, for they know not what they do." Not after the spitting, and the cursing, and the thorns, and the nails. Not if they don't care or understand that this horrible price in personal pain is being paid for them. But that is just the time when the fiercest kind of integrity and loyalty to high purpose must take over. That is just the time when it matters the very most and when everything else hangs in the balance—for surely it did that day. We won't ever find ourselves on that cross, but we repeatedly find ourselves at the foot of it. And how we act there will speak volumes about what we think of Christ's character and his call for us to be his disciples.

Our challenges will be a lot less dramatic than a tar-and-feathering; certainly they won't involve a crucifixion. And maybe they won't even be very personal matters at all. Maybe they will involve someone else — perhaps an injustice done to a neighbor, a person much less popular and privileged.

In cataloging life's little battles, this may be the least attractive kind of war for us, a bitter cup we especially don't wish to drink because there seems so little advantage in it for us. After all, it's really someone else's problem; and, like Hamlet, we may well lament that "time is out of joint; O cursed spite, / That ever [you were] born to set it right!" (*Hamlet*, Act I, sc. 5.) But set it right we must, for "inasmuch as ye have done it unto one of the least of these my brethren, ye have done it unto me." (Matthew 25:40.) And in times of such Doniphan-like defense, it may be risky, even dangerous, to stand true.

Martin Luther King once said, "The ultimate measure of a man is not where he stands in moments of comfort and convenience, but where he stands at times of challenge and controversy. The true neighbor will risk his position, his prestige, and even his life for the welfare of others. In dangerous valleys and hazardous pathways, he will lift some bruised and beaten brother to a higher and more noble life." (Martin Luther King, Jr., *Strength to Love* [New York: Harper and Row, 1963].)

But what if in this war it is neither a neighbor nor ourselves at risk, but someone desperately, dearly loved by us who is hurt or defamed or perhaps even taken in death? How might we prepare for that distant day when our own child, or our own spouse, is found in mortal danger?

One marvelously gifted man, a convert to Christianity, slowly watched his wife dying of cancer. As he observed her slipping away from him, with all that she had meant and had given him, his newfound faith about which he had written so much and with which he had strengthened so many others now began to waver. In times of such grief, C. S. Lewis wrote, one runs the risk of asking: "Where is God?' . . . When you are happy . . . [you] turn to Him with gratitude and praise, [and] you will be . . . welcomed with open arms. But go to

Him when your need is desperate, when all other help is vain, and what do you find? A door slammed in your face, and a sound of bolting and double bolting on the inside. After that, silence. You [might] as well turn away. The longer you wait, the more emphatic the silence will become. There are no lights in the windows. It might be an empty house. . . . [Yet he was once there.] What can this mean? Why is [God] so present a commander in our time of prosperity and so very absent a help in time of trouble?" (C. S. Lewis, *A Grief Observed* [New York: Seabury Press, 1961], pp. 4-5.)

Those feelings of abandonment, written in the midst of terrible grief, slowly passed, and the comfort of Lewis's faith returned, stronger and purer for the test. But note what self-revelation this bitter cup, this bloody baptism, had for him. In an obligation of quite a different kind, he too now realized that enlisting for the duration of the war is not a trivial matter, and in the heat of battle he hadn't been so heroic as he had encouraged millions of his readers to be.

"You never know how much you believe anything," he confessed, "until its truth or falsehood becomes a matter of life and death to you. It is easy to say you believe a rope to be strong and sound as long as you are merely using it to [tie] a box. But suppose you had to hang by that rope over a precipice. Wouldn't you then first discover how much you really trusted it? . . . Only a real risk tests the reality of a belief." (Ibid., p. 25.)

"Your [view of] . . . eternal life . . . will not be [very] serious if nothing much [is at] stake. . . . A man . . . has to be knocked silly before he comes to his senses." (Ibid., p. 43.)

"I had been warned — [indeed] I had warned myself. . . . [I knew] we were . . . promised sufferings. [That was] part of the program. We were even told, 'Blessed are they that mourn,' and I accepted it. I've got nothing that I hadn't [agreed to]. . . . [So] if my house . . . collapsed at one blow, that is because it was a house of cards. The faith which 'took these things into account' was not [an adequate]

161

faith. . . . If I had really cared, as I thought I did [care], about the sorrows of [others in this] world, [then] I should not have been so overwhelmed when my own sorrow came. . . . I thought I trusted the rope until it mattered. . . . [And when it indeed mattered, I found that it wasn't strong enough.]

" . . . You will never discover how serious it [is] until the stakes are raised horribly high; [and God has a way of raising the stakes] . . . [sometimes] only suffering [can] do [that]." (Ibid., pp. 41-43.)

"[So God is, then, something like a divine physician.] A cruel man might be bribed — might grow tired of his vile sport — might have a temporary fit of mercy, as alcoholics have [temporary] fits of sobriety. But suppose that what you are up against is a [wonderfully skilled] surgeon whose intentions are [solely and absolutely] good. [Then], the kinder and more conscientious he is, [the more he cares about you,] the more inexorably he will go on cutting [in spite of the suffering it may cause. And] if he yielded to your entreaties, if he stopped before the operation was complete, all the pain up to that point would have been useless. . . ." (Ibid., pp. 49-50.)

"[So I am, you see, one] of God's patients, not yet cured. I know there are not only tears [yet] to be dried but stains [yet] to be scoured. [My] sword will be made even brighter." (Ibid., p. 49.)

God wants us to be stronger than we are — more fixed in our purpose, more certain of our commitments, eventually needing less coddling from him, showing more willingness to shoulder some of the burden of his heavy load. In short, he wants us to be more like him.

The question, then, for all of us milling around the Greyhound Bus depot about to report for duty, is fundamental: When gospel principles get unpopular or unprofitable or difficult to live, will we stand by them "for the duration"? That is the question our experiences in Latter-day Saint life seem most determined to answer. What do we really believe, and how true to that are we really willing to live? As brothers and sisters, bright and blessed and eager and prosperous, do we yet know what faith—specifically faith in the Lord Jesus Christ—really is, what it requires in human behavior, and what it may yet demand of us before our souls are finally saved?

We must also remember that though the demands may be great, the blessings are even greater. Because of the Savior and his restored gospel, and because of the work of living prophets, there is for each of us a brilliant future of gospel promise. If we stay fixed and faithful in our purpose, there will be a great final moment somewhere when we will stand with the angels "in the presence of God, on a globe like a sea of glass and fire, where all things for [our] glory are manifest, past, present, and future." (D&C 130:7.)

That is the triumphant day that is promised, dependent upon our righteousness and for which we all dearly long. To earn the right to be there we must, as Alma said, "stand as witnesses of God at all times and in all things, and in all places that [we] may be in, even until death." (Mosiah 18:9.)

Chapter 14

WITHIN THE
CLASP OF YOUR ARMS

*If we wish our children to be taught the principles of the
gospel, if we wish them to love the truth and understand
it, if we wish them to be obedient to and united with us,
we must love them. And we must prove we love them
by our every word and act toward them.*

A recent study conducted by the Church has forcefully
confirmed statistically what we have been told again
and again. That is, if loving, inspired instruction
and example are not provided at home, then our related efforts
for success in and around Church programs are severely limited. It is increasingly clear that we must teach the gospel to
our families personally, live those teachings in our homes, or
run the risk of discovering too late that a Primary teacher or
priesthood adviser or seminary instructor *could* not do for our
children what we *would* not do for them.

May I offer just this much encouragement regarding such
a great responsibility? What I cherish in my relationship with
my son Matt is that he is, along with his mother and sister
and brother, my closest, dearest friend. I love to be with him.
We talk a lot. We laugh a lot. We play one-on-one basketball;
we play tennis and racquetball, though I do refuse to play
golf with him (that's a private joke). We discuss problems. I
am the president of a small university, and he is the president
of a large high school class. We compare notes and offer
suggestions and share each other's challenges. I pray for him

and have cried with him, and I'm immensely proud of him. We've talked long into the night lying on his waterbed, a twentieth-century aberration that I know, as part of the punishment of the last days, will one day burst and wash the Hollands helplessly into the streets of the city.

I feel I can talk to Matt about how he is enjoying seminary because I try to talk to him about all of his classes at school. We often imagine together what his mission will be like because he knows how much my mission meant to me. And he asks me about temple marriage because he knows I am absolutely crazy about his mother. He wants his future wife to be like her and for them to have what we have.

Now, I know that there are fathers and sons who feel they do not have any portion of what is here described. I know there are fathers who would give virtually their very lives to be close again to a struggling son. I know there are sons who wish their dads were at their side. I simply say to us all, young and old, never give up. Keep trying, keep reaching, keep talking, keep praying—but never give up. Above all, never pull away from each other.

May I share a brief but painful moment from my own efforts as a father.

Early in our married life my young family and I were laboring through graduate school at a university in New England. Pat was the Relief Society president in our ward, and I was serving in our stake presidency. I was going to school full-time and teaching half-time. We had two small children then, with little money and lots of pressures.

One evening I came home from long hours at school, feeling the proverbial weight of the world on my shoulders. Everything seemed to be especially demanding and discouraging and dark. I wondered if the dawn would ever come. Then, as I walked into our small student apartment, there was an unusual silence in the room.

"What's the trouble?" I asked.

"Matthew has something he wants to tell you," Pat said.

165

"Matt, what do you have to tell me?" He was quietly playing with his toys in the corner of the room, trying very hard not to hear me. "Matt," I said a little louder, "do you have something to tell me?"

He stopped playing, but for a moment he didn't look up. Then two enormous, tear-filled brown eyes turned toward me, and with the pain only a five-year-old can know, he said, "I didn't mind Mommy tonight, and I spoke back to her." With that he burst into tears, and his entire body shook with grief. A childish indiscretion had been noted, a painful confession had been offered, the growth of a five-year-old was continuing, and loving reconciliation could have been wonderfully underway.

Everything might have been just terrific—except for me. If you can imagine such an idiotic thing, I lost my temper. It wasn't that I lost it with Matt—it was with a hundred and one other things on my mind. But he didn't know that, and I wasn't disciplined enough to admit it. He got the whole load of bricks.

I told him how disappointed I was and how much more I thought I could have expected from him. I sounded like the parental pygmy I was. Then I did what I had never done before in his life: I told him that he was to go straight to bed and that I would not be in to say his prayers with him or to tell him a bedtime story. Muffling his sobs, he obediently went to his bedside, where he knelt—alone—to say his prayers. Then he stained his little pillow with tears his father should have been wiping away.

If you think the silence upon my arrival was heavy, you should have felt it now. Pat did not say a word. She didn't have to. I felt terrible!

Later, as we knelt by our own bed, my feeble prayer for blessings upon my family fell back on my ears with a horrible, hollow ring. I wanted to get up off my knees right then and go to Matt and ask his forgiveness, but he was long since peacefully asleep.

My own relief was not so soon coming, but finally I fell asleep and began to dream, which I seldom do. I dreamed Matt and I were packing two cars for a move. For some reason his mother and baby sister were not present. As we finished I turned to him and said, "Okay, Matt, you drive one car and I'll drive the other."

This five-year-old very obediently crawled up on the seat and tried to grasp the massive steering wheel. I walked over to the other car and started the motor. As I began to pull away, I looked to see how my son was doing. He was trying— oh, how he was trying. He tried to reach the pedals, but he couldn't. He was also turning knobs and pushing buttons, trying to start the motor. He could scarcely be seen over the dashboard, but there staring out at me again were those same immense, tear-filled, beautiful brown eyes. As I pulled away, he cried out, "Daddy, don't leave me. I don't know how to do it. I'm too little." And I drove away.

A short time later, driving down that desert road in my dream, I suddenly realized in one stark, horrifying moment what I had done. I slammed my car to a stop, threw open the door, and started to run as fast as I could. I left car, keys, belongings, and all—and I ran. The pavement was so hot it burned my feet, and tears blinded my straining effort to see this child somewhere on the horizon. I kept running, praying, pleading to be forgiven and to find my boy safe and secure.

As I rounded a curve, nearly ready to drop from physical and emotional exhaustion, I saw the unfamiliar car I had left Matt to drive. It was pulled carefully off to the side of the road, and he was laughing and playing nearby. An older man was with him, playing and responding to his games. Matt saw me and cried out something like, "Hi, Dad. We're having fun." Obviously he had already forgiven and forgotten my terrible transgression against him.

But I dreaded the older man's gaze, which followed my every move. I tried to say "Thank you," but his eyes were filled with sorrow and disappointment. I muttered an awkward apology and the stranger said simply, "You should not have left him alone to do this difficult thing. It would not have been asked of you."

With that, the dream ended, and I shot upright in bed. My pillow was stained, whether with perspiration or tears I do not know. I threw off the covers and ran to the little metal camp cot that was my son's bed. There on my knees and through my tears I cradled him in my arms and spoke to him while he slept. I told him that every dad makes mistakes but that they don't mean to. I told him it wasn't his fault I had had a bad day. I told him that when boys are five or fifteen, dads sometimes forget and think they are fifty. I told him that I wanted him to be a small boy for a long, long time, because all too soon he would grow up and be a man and wouldn't be playing on the floor with his toys when I came home. I told him that I loved him and his mother and his sister more than anything in the world, and that whatever challenges we had in life, we would face them together. I told him that never again would I withhold my affection or my forgiveness from him, and never, I prayed, would he withhold them from me. I told him I was honored to be his father and that I would try with all my heart to be worthy of such a great responsibility.

Well, I have not proven to be the perfect father I vowed to be that night and a thousand nights before and since. But I still want to be, and I believe this wise counsel from President Joseph F. Smith: "Brethren, . . . If you will keep your [children] close to your heart, within the clasp of your arms; if you will make them to feel that you love them, . . . and keep them near to you, they will not go very far from you, and they will not commit any very great sin. But it is when you turn them out of the home, turn them out of your affection . . . that [is what] drives them from you. . . .

"Fathers, if you wish your children to be taught in the principles of the gospel, if you wish them to love the truth and understand it, if you wish them to be obedient to and united with you, love them! and prove to them that you do love them by your every word and act to[ward] them." (*Gospel Doctrine*, 5th ed. [Salt Lake City: Deseret Book, 1966], pp. 282, 316.)

We all know fatherhood is not an easy assignment, but it ranks among the most imperative assignments ever given, in time or eternity. We must not pull away from our children. We must keep trying, keep reaching, keep praying, keep listening. We must keep them "within the clasp of our arms." That is what fathers are for.

Chapter 15

WHO WE ARE
AND WHAT GOD
EXPECTS US TO DO

Education is to help us learn who we really are and discover what God expects us to do. One thing he expects us to remember is that we are heirs of a gospel dispensation that had among its earliest commandments the challenge to "seek . . . diligently and teach one another words of wisdom; yea, seek . . . out of the best books . . . learning, even by study and also by faith." God's glory is intelligence, and it is to be our glory as well.

At least one writer believes that most of what we need to know was suggested to us more than a dozen years ago. Given the costs of a university education, such an assertion is worth investigating. Consider his argument:

"Most of what I really need to know about how to live, and what to do, and how to be I learned in kindergarten. Wisdom was not at the top of the graduate-school mountain, but there in the sandbox.

"These are the things I learned: Share everything. Play fair. Don't hit people. Put things back where you found them. Clean up your own mess. Don't take things that aren't yours. Say you're sorry when you hurt somebody. Wash your hands before you eat. Live a balanced life. Learn some and think some, and draw and sing and dance and play and work every day some.

"Take a nap in the afternoon. When you go out into the

world, watch for traffic, hold hands and stick together. Be aware of wonder. Remember the little seed in the plastic cup. The roots go down and the plant goes up, and nobody really knows why, but we are all like that.

"Goldfish and hamsters and white mice and even the little seed in the plastic cup—they all die. So do we.

"And then remember the book about Dick and Jane and the first word you learned, the biggest word of all: look. Everything you need to know is in there somewhere. The golden rule and love and basic sanitation. Ecology and politics and sane living.

"Think of what a better world it would be if we all had cookies and milk about three o'clock every afternoon and then lay down with our blankets for a nap. Or if we had a basic policy in our nation and other nations always to put things back where we found them and cleaned up our own messes. And it is still true, no matter how old you are, when you go out into the world, it is best to hold hands and stick together." (Robert Fulghum, "We Learned It All in Kindergarten," *Reader's Digest*, October 1987, p. 115.)

I admit that is a pretty good list, whether one is five or fifty. In fact, maybe *most* of the important things we need to hear in life have long since been said to us—probably many times. The inestimable Samuel Johnson once said that people needed reminding far more than they needed instructing, so may I share some reminders largely drawn from the past.

But preserving our past without compromising the present is often no easy matter—it can put us in a precarious position, something like, well, a fiddler on the roof. In fact, I wish to invoke Tevye's help in recounting and reminding us of truths taught to most of us since kindergarten and before. Here's Tevye on "tradition":

"A fiddler on the roof. Sounds crazy, no? But in our little village of Anatevka, you might say every one of us is a fiddler on the roof, trying to scratch out a pleasant, simple tune without breaking his neck. It isn't easy. You may ask, why do we stay up here if it's so dangerous? We stay because Anatevka is our home. And how do we keep our balance? That I can tell you in a word—tradition!

"Because of our traditions, we've kept our balance for many, many years. Here in Anatevka we have traditions for everything—how to eat, how to sleep, how to wear clothes. For instance, we always keep our heads covered and always wear a little prayer shawl. This shows our constant devotion to God. You may ask, how did this tradition start? I'll tell you—I don't know! But it's a tradition. Because of our traditions, everyone knows who he is and what God expects him to do." ("Fiddler on the Roof," in *Great Musicals of the American Theatre,* ed. Stanley Richards, vol. 1 [Radnor, Pennsylvania: Chilton Book Company, 1973], p. 393.)

Who are we, then? And what does God expect us to do? For one thing, he expects us to remember we are heirs of a gospel dispensation that had among its earliest commandments the challenge to "seek . . . diligently and teach one another words of wisdom; yea, seek . . . out of the best books . . . learning, even by study and also by faith." (D&C 88:118; see also D&C 88:78.) This crucial commandment is inextricably linked with the profound restored truth that teaches us we are literally sons and daughters of God and that we can someday become like him. Restored truth teaches that God's glory is his intelligence and that it is to be our glory as well.

That inestimable doctrine, restored to a darkened world more than a century and a half ago, has in that length of time developed into a strong tradition for Latter-day Saints, the earliest of whom labored by day and read books by night in an effort to become more like God "by study and also by faith."

It is not insignificant that the central symbol and only tract of their early faith was a book, a written record that would give meaning to all they did and to everything they believed. No one had to tell *them* the importance of reading; it was a "habit of the heart." Later they would gather in the upper room of their Ohio temple to study not only theology but also mathematics, philosophy, English grammar, geography, and Hebrew. And on the banks of the Mississippi they would plan Nauvoo, the City Beautiful, their Zion-like city/state, around two great centers of learning — a temple and a university. Even when driven from their homes, the Saints kept the dream alive. In dugouts and cabins, handcarts and Conestogas, school was held. It was not easy but it was doctrine. "It is impossible . . . to be saved in ignorance," their prophet-teacher had said, and "Whatever principle of intelligence we attain unto in this life, it will rise with us in the resurrection." (D&C 131:6; 130:18.) They believed him. They were as hungry as Erasmus, a philosopher in the sixteenth century who wrote, "When I get a little money, I buy books; and if any is left [over], I buy [bread]."

"Wherever Mormon settlements have sprung up the village school has been among the first things thought of and provided for," said future president of the Church Lorenzo Snow. In those parts of the new Mormon territory where buildings were not available, schoolteachers simply did the best they could. Said Elder George A. Smith of his experience in southern Utah, "My wicky-up is a very important establishment, composed of brush, a few slabs and 3 wagons. [It has a] fire in the center and a lot of milking stools, benches and logs placed around, two of which are fashioned with buffalo robes. . . . [It was, however, unpleasant] to see my school some of the cold nights in February, scholars standing round my huge camp fire, the wind broken off by the brush and the whole canopy of heaven for covering. Thermometer standing at 7! . . . I would stand with my grammar book, the only one in school, would give out a sentence at a time and pass it around." (Ernest L. Wilkinson and W. Cleon Skousen, *Brigham Young University: A School of Destiny* [Provo, Utah: Brigham Young University Press, 1976], p. 15.)

Out of that tradition for learning, that near-unquenchable

thirst for knowledge, has come Brigham Young University—
a far cry from milking stools, buffalo robes, and one text; a
far cry from what a century of our pioneer ancestors fought
for and dreamed of but for the most part did not live long
enough to see.

We owe them something. We who are the beneficiaries of
their sacrifice and their faith—we owe them the best effort
we can put forward in obtaining a truly edifying and liberating
and spirit-soaring education. We need to work hard, take
advantage of every opportunity, play a lot less and study a
lot more. We need to learn to write and speak well, and make
an investment in ourselves the way the tithe payers of the
Church have made one in us, and see that bread cast upon
academic waters come back to us and our posterity a hun-
dredfold. Let us load our handcarts full of books and start off
for Zion, and go forward in the same way our ancestors went
forward—often with nothing more tangible to sustain them
than their dreams and their traditions.

"The glory of God." "Light and truth." Most of us have
heard all of that since kindergarten or before. The question
for us now is, "What will we do with this ideal?" Remember
Anatevka. "Everyone knows who he is and what God expects
him to do." Tradition!

Closely linked with that latter-day pursuit of learning is
another important tradition. The first year I came to the university as president I coined a homely Latin phrase, *virtus et
veritas,* to define a twofold mission. I added to the search for
veritas (truth) a second task, *virtus* (virtue), believing with all
my heart that how one lived was the ultimate test of an education, that truth standing undefended or unexercised was
unworthy of the investment that had gone into her discovery.

In doing so I knew I had not only the philosophers but
also the prophets of God, past and present, on my side. Indeed, a modern First Presidency of the Church said this in a
better way than most professional educators would ever say

174

it. Said Brigham Young, Heber C. Kimball, and Willard Richards:

"If men [and we would add women] would be great in goodness, they must be intelligent, for no man can do good unless he knows how; therefore seek after knowledge, all knowledge, and especially that which is from above, which is wisdom to direct in all things, and if you find any thing that God does not know, you need not learn that thing; but strive to know what God knows, and use that knowledge as God uses it, and then you will be like him; [you] will . . . have charity, love one another, and do each other good continually, and for ever. . . . But if a man have all knowledge, and does not use it for good, it will prove a curse instead of a blessing as it did to Lucifer, the Son of the Morning." (Millennial Star 14 [January 15, 1852]: 22.)

What a striking educational philosophy! It sounds so simple: learn and love, strive to know what God knows, use that knowledge as God uses it, and you will be like him. Strive for education to do each other good continually and forever. But of course that was first taught to us in our kindergarten years. Play fair. Don't hit. Clean up your own mess. Hold hands and stick together. Our education has always carried with it ineluctable moral obligations.

How important is all of this as we balance precariously on the roof? Very important, I think. As a nation we are swirling in — and seemingly overwhelmed by — ethical and cultural and political chaos. The moral implications for our society, as severe as any America has faced, are serious partly because they directly threaten the very idea of society. These violations of the commonweal damage our efforts to live together in trust and reciprocity.

"The United States needs to recover some idealism," read one recent newspaper headline. "Universities are turning out highly skilled barbarians," trumpets a national news magazine. We are a "nation without honor," declares a monthly periodical; a "nation of liars," cries another. Even the Pope travels to America to remind us of our lost virtues. And no less an arbiter of national virtue than *Time* magazine runs a cover story on "sleaze, scandals and hypocrisy," documenting the nation's frenzied search for its values, a mad scramble for bearings in a time of stunning moral disarray.

University students have also contributed their share to the general morass. Consider this from a recent educational quarterly:

"Popular literature has painted today's generation of college students as a cynical bunch of money-grubbers, willing to stoop to any level to 'get ahead.' . . . Sadly enough, . . . students [today do] not cherish or even understand the basic principles of academic honesty. The evidence, based almost entirely on self-reporting, shows clearly that the levels of [university] cheating are high. . . . The picture . . . is of a self-centered, competitive, insecure, and cynical generation of students, committed to getting the most out of the present [regardless of the cost to others]. In this context, it is not surprising that colleges and universities are becoming concerned about the ethical standards of their students." (Richard A. Fass, "By Honor Bound: Encouraging Academic Honesty," *Educational Record,* Fall 1986, p. 32.)

Becoming concerned? "The ethical standards of their students" is not just a trendy issue in the Church. It is our heritage, our tradition. And it should be a tradition at every university. But quite frankly, universities that exist only as universities can't do it. As Hitler rose to power and forged the infamy of the Third Reich, Germany had the finest university tradition in all of continental Europe. And most of the truly desperate and severe problems I have referred to in America — whether moral, political, or cultural — have come at the hands of university-trained men and women. (I intentionally use the word *trained* rather than *educated.*) No, "full and fair intellectual inquiry" alone won't do it. Academic instruction unmeasured and untempered by integrity, instruction unenlightened by the civilizing forces and moral obligations that go with the truth, will simply produce ever more "highly skilled barbarians." And almost any newspaper or nightly news broadcast can show us plenty of those. Remember, "If a man have all knowledge, and does not use it for good, it will prove a curse instead of a blessing as it did to Lucifer, the Son of the Morning."

Of course, the saddest element in all of this for me is not that the world doesn't understand civilizing values or, worse yet, that educationists often don't, but saddest of all is that some Latter-day Saints don't seem to get it either—even with long-established and frequently repeated traditions to guide us. The infractions of those very few then often damage the experience and opportunity of others.

It goes without saying that Latter-day Saints bear a special burden because we point out we are different, because we say we stand for something traditional and spiritually worthwhile. Of course the moment we say that, we are marked women and men—there are multitudes who would love to bring us down. But that's all right; it's just all the more reason for us, after cookie and milk time, to hold hands and stick together.

By the time we come to a university we've had adequate time to consider this shared sense of responsibility we have for life lived together. The Declaration of Independence of the United States declares that democracy rightly lived requires a commitment no less than "our lives, our fortunes, and our sacred honor," as Thomas Jefferson finally phrased it. I'd like to think that in some modest way our "gamble" in the twentieth century on the virtue and morality and integrity of young men and women is not unlike America's gamble in the eighteenth. Ben Franklin spoke for all of us when he said at that fateful signing on July 4, 1776, "We must all hang together, or assuredly we shall all hang separately."

We don't have to quote John Donne at this point to remember that no man is an island. Everyone who enters an LDS university has, in a rather literal way, entered a covenantal society. We take our position on the roof, with violin in hand, and we declare to the rest of the world, "Tradition."

Tradition? Tradition! A lot of it, dearly earned and even more dearly defended. It's tough keeping our footing on a slippery roof, but there we are, determined to stay. The only way we can succeed is through the integrity and the disciplined behavior of our citizens who voluntarily choose to live in a rigorously disciplined society. Each of us must be true to Christ and our covenants. In an age when culture is about five miles wide and three-sixteenths of an inch deep, I ask for something deeper. I want an inspiring past, present, and future—in short, a tradition—that will give depth and height and millennia of meaning to individuals. That will only come from our understanding of the glory of God and our determination to enjoy fully his blessings to us.

Do you remember the seed and the cup from the kindergarten story? "The roots go down and the plant goes up, and nobody really knows why." I want our roots down and our plants up—and the more visible those stems and branches and blossoms are, the deeper our roots will have to go to sustain them. Let's not get caught in shallow soil, intellectually or spiritually. The Savior taught powerful parables about seeds needing to be planted deeply and houses needing to be built on strong foundations.

Let me conclude with a story about tradition. Karl G. Maeser was certainly one of the most refined and educated men to join The Church of Jesus Christ of Latter-day Saints in the first fifty years of its restored existence. Trained in the great classical tradition and distinguished in Saxony for his breadth of learning, he gave up virtually everything he had to enter the waters of baptism. Ostracized in his community and with no way to make a living, he brought his wife and two children to America, serving missions as he came and finally joining the Saints in the valleys of the Rocky Mountains. He then gave the rest of his life to the educational efforts of the Church, including fifteen years in abject poverty as the first and greatest principal of the then new and struggling Brigham Young Academy in Provo, Utah.

In December 1900, two months before he died, Brother Maeser was brought back to see once more the modest single-building campus on University Avenue he had built and loved and defended. He was helped up the stairs and into one of the classrooms, where the students instinctively stood as he entered. Not a word was spoken. He looked at them, then slowly made his way to the chalkboard. With his bold classical script he wrote four statements on the board, then walked out of the school forever, closing as he did so perhaps one of the most distinguished lives the university has ever known.

Several years after Brother Maeser's death a proposal was made to construct a memorial building in his name, not downtown on University Avenue but high atop Temple Hill, where a new campus might be built consisting of as many as three or perhaps four buildings someday. The cost would be an astronomical $100,000, but the Maeser Building would be a symbol of the past, a statement of aspiring tradition, an anchor to the university's future.

In spite of a staggering financial crisis clouding the very future of the university at the time, the faculty and student body took heart that in 1912 the Maeser Building was at least partially complete and the university would give diplomas to its first four-year graduating class. But even as graduation plans were being made, equally urgent plans were underway to sell the remainder of Temple Hill for the development of a new Provo suburb. The university simply had to have the money to survive. Eighteen members were graduating in this first four-year class, but even if the student body tripled in the years ahead, surely there would be more than enough room to accommodate them on the space now occupied by the Maeser, Brimhall, and Grant buildings on our present campus. Yes, the rest of the space on the hill should be sold. The graduation services would conclude with a sales pitch to the community leaders in attendance.

When Alfred Kelly was introduced that morning as the student graduation speaker, he rose and stood absolutely silent for several moments. Some in the audience thought he had lost the power of speech. Slowly he began to speak, explaining that he had been so concerned about his remarks that he had written several versions and discarded every one of them. Then, early one morning, he said, with a feeling of desperation regarding his approaching assignment, he walked north from his downtown apartment to where the partially completed Maeser Building stood (as Horace Cummings would later describe it) as an "air castle" come to earth on Temple Hill. He wanted to gain inspiration from this hope of a new campus, but he felt only grim disappointment. The sky was starting to glow from the morning light, but the darkly silhouetted Maeser Building seemed only a symbol of gloom.

Kelly then turned his eyes to view the valley below, which was also still in shadow. The light from the rising sun was just beginning to illuminate the western hills back of Utah Lake with an unusual golden glow. As morning came, the light gradually worked down from the hilltops, moved across the valley floor, and slowly advanced to where Kelly stood.

He said he partially closed his eyes as the light approached and was startled by what he could see. He stood as if transfixed. In the advancing sunlight everything he saw took on the appearance of people, young people about his age moving toward Temple Hill. He saw hundreds of them, thousands of young people coming into view. He knew they were students, he said, because they carried books in their arms as they came.

Then Temple Hill was bathed in sunlight, and the whole of the present campus was illuminated not with one partially completed building, nor with homes in a modern subdivision, but rather with what Kelly described to that graduating class as "temples of learning," large buildings, beautiful buildings, hundreds of buildings covering the top of that hill and stretching clear to the mouth of Rock Canyon.

The students then entered those temples of learning with their books in hand. As they came out of the buildings, Kelly said, their countenances bore smiles of hope and of faith. He observed that they seemed cheerful and very confident. Their walk was light but firm as they again became a part of the sunlight moving to the top of Y Mountain, and then they gradually disappeared from view.

Kelly sat down to what was absolutely stone-deaf silence. Not a word was spoken. What about the sales pitch? No one moved or whispered. Then long-time BYU benefactor Jesse Knight jumped to his feet and shouted, "We won't sell an acre. We won't sell a single lot." And he turned to President George Brimhall and pledged several thousand dollars to the future of the university. Soon others stood up and joined in, some offering only a widow's mite, but all believing in the dream of a Provo school boy, all believing in the destiny of a great university which that day had scarcely begun. (B. F. Larsen, speech to BYU Alumni, May 25, 1962.)

Consider now a campus that now stretches from that newly renovated Maeser Building to the very mouth of Rock Canyon itself, where a special temple of learning, built on BYU property, watches by night and day over Utah Valley. Think of the buildings and think of the lives and think of the tradition.

Oh, yes. I suppose you are wondering about those four things Karl G. Maeser wrote on the board that day. They are part of the tradition, too:

1. [To love] God is the beginning of all wisdom.

2. This life is one great [homework] assignment . . . in the principles of immortality and eternal life.

3. Man grows only with his higher goals.

4. Never let anything impure enter here.

A fiddler on the roof? It's a tough assignment, but we are all in it together, defending that inheritance. May we discover in our tradition of learning and love and purity who we really are and what God expects us to do.

181

Chapter 16

OF SOULS, SYMBOLS,
AND SACRAMENTS

*The spirit and the body constitute the soul of man. We
should look upon this body as something that shall endure
beyond the grave, something to be kept pure and holy.
Be not afraid of soiling its hands nor of scars that may
come in earnest effort, but beware of scars that come in
places you ought not to have gone. Beware of the wounds
of battles in which you have been fighting on the wrong
side.*

The topic of human intimacy is as sacred as any I know.
In discussing it, the subject can slide quickly from the
sacred into the merely sensational. It would be better
not to address the topic at all than to damage it with casualness
or carelessness.

Some may feel this is a topic we hear discussed too frequently, but given the world in which we live, we may not
be hearing it enough. All of the prophets, past and present,
have spoken on it. Most in the Church are doing wonderfully
well in the matter of personal purity but some are not doing
so well, and much of the world around us is not doing well
at all.

In 1987 the national press noted, "In America 3,000 ad-
olescents become pregnant each day. A million a year. Four
out of five are unmarried. More than half get abortions. 'Babies
having babies.' [Babies] killing [babies]." ("What's Gone
Wrong with Teen Sex," *People*, April 13, 1987, p. 111.)

That same national poll indicated that nearly 60 percent of high school students in "mainstream" America had lost their virginity, and 80 percent of college students had. A writer for *The Wall Street Journal* wrote, "AIDS [appears to be reaching] plague[-like] proportions. Even now it is claiming innocent victims: newborn babies and recipients of blood transfusions. It is only a matter of time before it becomes widespread among heterosexuals. . . . AIDS should remind us that ours is a hostile world. . . . The more we pass ourselves around, the larger the likelihood of our picking something up. . . . Whether on clinical or moral grounds, it seems clear that promiscuity has its price." (May 21, 1987, p. 28.)

Of course, more widespread in our society than the indulgence of personal sexual activity are the printed and photographed descriptions of those who do so indulge. Of that lustful environment a contemporary observer says, "We live in an age in which voyeurism is no longer the side line of the solitary deviate, but rather a national pastime, fully institutionalized and [circularized] in the mass media." (William F. May, quoted by Henry Fairlie, *The Seven Deadly Sins Today* [Notre Dame, Indiana: University of Notre Dame Press, 1978], p. 178.)

In fact, the rise of civilization seems, ironically enough, to have made actual or fantasized promiscuity a greater, not a lesser, problem. Edward Gibbon, the distinguished British historian of the eighteenth century, wrote, "Although the progress of civilisation has undoubtedly contributed to assuage the fiercer passions of human nature, it seems to have been less favourable to the virtue of chastity. . . . The refinements of life [seem to] corrupt, [even as] they polish, the [relationship] of the sexes." *(The Decline and Fall of the Roman Empire*, vol. 40 of *Great Books of the Western World*, 1952, p. 92.)

But it is useless to document social problems or wring our hands over the dangers that such outside influences may hold for us. As serious as such contemporary realities are, I wish to discuss this topic in quite a different way, discuss it specifically for Latter-day Saints. I conspicuously set aside the horrors of AIDS and national statistics on illegitimate pregnancies and refer rather to a gospel-based view of personal purity.

Indeed, I wish to do something even a bit more difficult than listing the do's and don'ts of personal purity. I wish to examine, to the best of my ability, *why* we should be clean, *why* moral discipline is such a significant matter in God's eyes. I know that may sound presumptuous, but a philosopher once said, "Tell me sufficiently why a thing should be done, and I will move heaven and earth to do it." Hoping you will feel the same way as he, and with full recognition of my limitations, I wish to try to give at least a partial answer to "Why be morally clean?" I will need first to pose briefly what I see as the doctrinal seriousness of the matter before then offering just three reasons for such seriousness.

May I begin with one-half of a nine-line poem by Robert Frost. (The other half is worth a sermon also, but it will have to wait for another day.) Here are the first four lines of Frost's "Fire and Ice": "Some say the world will end in fire, / Some say in ice. / From what I've tasted of desire / I hold with those who favor fire."

A second, less poetic but more specific opinion is offered by the writer of Proverbs: "Can a man take fire in his bosom, and his clothes not be burned? Can one go upon hot coals, and his feet not be burned? . . . But whoso committeth adultery with a woman lacketh understanding: he that doeth it destroyeth his own soul. A wound and dishonour shall he get; and his reproach shall not be wiped away." (Proverbs 6:27-28, 32-33.)

In getting at the doctrinal seriousness, why is this matter of sexual relationships so severe that fire is almost always the metaphor, with passion pictured vividly in flames? What is there in the potentially hurtful heat of this that leaves one's soul—or perhaps the whole world, according to Frost—destroyed, if that flame is left unchecked and those passions

184

unrestrained? What is there in all of this that prompts Alma to warn his son Corianton that sexual transgression is "an abomination in the sight of the Lord; yea, most abominable above *all* sins save it be the shedding of innocent blood or denying the Holy Ghost"? (Alma 39:5. Italics added.)

Setting aside sins against the Holy Ghost for a moment as a special category unto themselves, it is LDS doctrine that sexual transgression is second only to murder in the Lord's list of life's most serious sins. By assigning such rank to a physical appetite so conspicuously evident in all of us, what is God trying to tell us about its place in his plan for all men and women in mortality? I submit to you he is doing precisely that—commenting about the very plan of life itself. Clearly God's greatest concerns regarding mortality are how one gets into this world and how one gets out of it. These two most important issues in our very personal and carefully supervised progress are the two issues that he as our Creator and Father and Guide wishes most to reserve to himself. These are the two matters that he has repeatedly told us he wants us never to take illegally, illicitly, unfaithfully, without sanction.

As for the *taking* of life, we are generally quite responsible. Most people, it seems to me, readily sense the sanctity of life and as a rule do not run up to friends, put a loaded revolver to their heads, and cavalierly pull the trigger. Furthermore, when there is a click of the hammer rather than an explosion of lead, and a possible tragedy seems to have been averted, no one in such a circumstance would be so stupid as to sigh, "Oh, good. I didn't go all the way."

No, "all the way" or not, the insanity of such action with fatal powder and steel is obvious on the face of it. Such a person running about with an arsenal of loaded handguns or military weaponry aimed at young people would be appre-hended, prosecuted, and institutionalized if in fact such a lunatic would not himself have been killed in all the pande-monium. After such a fictitious moment of horror, we would undoubtedly sit in our homes or classrooms with terror on

185

our minds for many months to come, wondering how such a thing could possibly happen—especially to members of the Church.

Fortunately, in the case of how life is taken, I think we seem to be quite responsible. The seriousness of that does not often have to be spelled out, and not many sermons need to be devoted to it. But in the significance and sanctity of *giving* life, some of us are not so responsible, and in the larger world swirling around us we find near-criminal irresponsibility. What would in the case of taking life bring absolute horror and demand grim justice, in the case of giving life brings dirty jokes and four-letter lyrics and crass carnality on the silver screen, home-owned or downtown.

Is all of this so wrong? That question has always been asked, usually by the guilty. "Such is the way of an adulterous woman; she eateth, and wipeth her mouth, and saith, I have done no wickedness." (Proverbs 30:20.) No murder here. Well, maybe not. But sexual transgression? "He that doeth it destroyeth his own soul." (Proverbs 6:32.) Sounds near fatal to me.

So much for the doctrinal seriousness. Now, with a desire to prevent such painful moments, to avoid what Alma called the "inexpressible horror" of standing in the presence of God unworthily, and to permit the intimacy it is your right and privilege and delight to enjoy in marriage to be untainted by such crushing remorse and guilt—I wish to give those three reasons I mentioned earlier as to why I believe this is an issue of such magnitude and consequence.

First, we simply must understand the revealed, restored Latter-day Saint doctrine of the soul, and the high and inextricable part the body plays in that doctrine.

One of the "plain and precious" truths restored to this dispensation is that "the spirit *and* the body are the soul of man" (D&C 88:15; italics added), and that when the spirit and body are separated, men and women "cannot receive a fulness of joy" (D&C 93:34). Certainly that suggests something of the reason why obtaining a body is so fundamentally important to the plan of salvation in the first place, why sin of any kind is such a serious matter (namely, because its automatic consequence is death, the separation of the spirit from the body and the separation of the spirit and the body from God), and why the resurrection of the body is so central to the great abiding and eternal triumph of Christ's atonement. We do not have to be a herd of demonically possessed swine charging down the Gadarene slopes toward the sea to understand that a body is *the* great prize of mortal life, and that even a pig's will do for those frenzied spirits that rebelled and that to this day remain dispossessed, in their first, unembodied estate.

May I quote a 1913 sermon by Elder James E. Talmage on this doctrinal point:

"We have been taught . . . to look upon these bodies of ours as gifts from God. We Latter-day Saints do not regard the body as something to be condemned, something to be abhorred. . . . We regard [the body] as a sign of our royal birthright. . . . We recognize the fact that those who kept not their first estate . . . were denied that inestimable blessing. . . . We believe that these bodies . . . may be made, in very truth, the temple of the Holy Ghost. . . .

"It is peculiar to the theology of the Latter-day Saints that we regard the body as an essential part of the soul. Read your dictionaries, the lexicons, and encyclopedias, and you will find that nowhere, outside of the Church of Jesus Christ, is the solemn and eternal truth taught that the soul of man is the body and the spirit combined." (*Conference Report*, October 1913, p. 117.)

So partly in answer to *why* such seriousness, we answer that one who toys with the God-given—and satanically coveted—body of another toys with the very soul of that individual, toys with the central purpose and product of life, "the very key" to life, as Elder Boyd K. Packer once called it. In trivializing the soul of another (please include the word *body* there) we trivialize the atonement which saved that soul and

187

guaranteed its continued existence. And when one toys with the Son of Righteousness, the Day Star himself, one toys with white heat and a flame hotter and holier than the noonday sun. You cannot do so and not be burned. You cannot with impunity "crucify . . . the Son of God afresh." (Hebrews 6:6.) Exploitation of the body (please include the word *soul* there) is, in the last analysis, an exploitation of him who is the Light and the Life of the world. Perhaps here, Paul's warning to the Corinthians takes on newer, higher meaning:

"Now the body is not for fornication, but for the Lord; and the Lord for the body. . . . Know ye not that your bodies are the members of Christ? shall I then take the members of Christ, and make them the members of an harlot? God forbid. . . . Flee fornication. . . . He that committeth fornication sinneth against his own body. What? know ye not that your body is the temple of the Holy Ghost which is in you, which ye have of God, and *ye are not your own?* . . . For ye are bought with a price: therefore glorify God *in your body, and in your spirit,* which are God's." (1 Corinthians 6:13-20. Italics added.)

Our soul is what is at stake here—our spirit *and* our body. Paul understood that doctrine of the soul every bit as well as James E. Talmage did, because it is gospel truth. The purchase price for our fullness of joy—body and spirit eternally united—is the pure and innocent blood of the Savior of the world. We cannot then say in ignorance or defiance, "Well, it's my life" or worse yet, "It's my body." It is *not.* "Ye are not your own," Paul said. "Ye are bought with a price." So in answer to the question, "Why does God care so much about sexual transgression?" it is partly because of the precious gift offered by and through his Only Begotten Son to redeem the souls—bodies *and* spirits—we too often share and abuse in such cheap and tawdry ways. Christ restored the very seeds of eternal lives (see D&C 132:19, 24), and we desecrate them at our peril. The first key reason for personal purity? Our very souls are involved and at stake.

Second, human intimacy, that sacred, physical union ordained of God for a married couple, deals with a symbol that demands special sanctity.

Such an act of love between a man and a woman is—or certainly was ordained to be—a symbol of total union: union of their hearts, their hopes, their lives, their love, their family, their future, their everything. It is a symbol that we try to suggest in the temple with a word like *seal*. The Prophet Joseph Smith once said we perhaps ought to render such a sacred bond as *welding*—that those united in matrimony and eternal families are *welded* together, inseparable if you will, to withstand the temptations of the adversary and the afflictions of mortality. (See D&C 128:18.)

But such a total, virtually unbreakable union, such an unyielding commitment between a man and a woman, can come only with the proximity and permanence afforded in a marriage covenant, with the union of all that they possess— their very hearts and minds, all their days and all their dreams. They work together, they cry together, they enjoy Brahms and Beethoven and breakfast together, they sacrifice and save and live together for all the abundance that such a totally intimate life provides such a couple. And the external symbol of that union, the physical manifestation of what is a far deeper spiritual and metaphysical bonding, is the physical blending that is part of—indeed, a most beautiful and gratifying expression of—that larger, more complete union of eternal purpose and promise.

As delicate as it is to mention, I nevertheless trust the reader's maturity to understand that physiologically we are created as men and women to form such a union. In this ultimate physical expression of one man and one woman, they are as nearly and as literally one as two separate physical bodies can ever be. It is in that act of ultimate physical intimacy that we most nearly fulfill the commandment of the Lord given to Adam and Eve, living symbols for all married couples, when

189

he invited them to cleave unto one another only, and thus become "one flesh." (Genesis 2:24.)

Obviously, such a commandment to these two, the first husband and wife of the human family, has unlimited implications—social, cultural and religious as well as physical—but that is exactly my point. As all couples come to that moment of bonding in mortality, it is to be just such a complete union. That commandment cannot be fulfilled, and that symbolism of "one flesh" cannot be preserved, if we hastily and guiltily and surreptitiously share intimacy in a darkened corner of a darkened hour, then just as hastily and guiltily and surreptitiously retreat to our separate worlds—not to eat or live or cry or laugh together, not to do the laundry and the dishes and the homework, not to manage a budget and pay the bills and tend the children and plan together for the future. No, we cannot do that until we are truly one—united, bound, linked, tied, welded, sealed, married.

Can you see then the moral schizophrenia that comes from pretending we are one, sharing the physical symbols and physical intimacy of our union, but then fleeing, retreating, severing all such other aspects—and symbols—of what was meant to be a total obligation, only to unite again furtively some other night or, worse yet, furtively unite (and you can tell how cynically I use that word) with some other partner who is no more bound to us, no more one with us than the last was or than the one that will come next week or next month or next year or anytime before the binding commitments of marriage?

You must wait until you can give everything, and you cannot give everything until you are at least legally and, for Latter-day Saint purposes, eternally pronounced as one. To give illicitly that which is not yours to give (remember, "you are not your own") and to give only part of that which cannot be followed with the gift of your whole heart and your whole life and your whole self is its own form of emotional Russian roulette. If you persist in sharing part without the whole, in pursuing satisfaction devoid of symbolism, in giving parts and pieces and inflamed fragments only, you run the terrible risk of such spiritual, psychic damage that you may undermine both your physical intimacy and your wholehearted devotion to a truer, later love. You may come to that moment of real love, of total union, only to discover to your horror that what you should have saved has been spent and that only God's grace can recover that piecemeal dissipation of your virtue.

A good Latter-day Saint friend, Dr. Victor L. Brown, Jr., has written of this issue:

"Fragmentation enables its users to counterfeit intimacy. . . . If we relate to each other in fragments, at best we miss full relationships. At worst, we manipulate and exploit others for our gratification. Sexual fragmentation can be particularly harmful because it gives powerful physiological rewards which, though illusory, can temporarily persuade us to overlook the serious deficits in the overall relationship. Two people may marry for physical gratification and then discover that the illusion of union collapses under the weight of intellectual, social, and spiritual incompatibilities. . . .

"Sexual fragmentation is particularly harmful because it is particularly deceptive. The intense human intimacy that should be enjoyed in and symbolized by sexual union is counterfeited by sensual episodes which suggest—but cannot deliver—acceptance, understanding, and love. Such encounters mistake the end for the means as lonely, desperate people seek a common denominator which will permit the easiest, quickest gratification." *(Human Intimacy: Illusion & Reality* [Salt Lake City: Parliament Publishers, 1981], pp. 5-6.)

Listen to a far more biting observation by a non-Latter-day Saint regarding such acts devoid of both the soul and the symbolism we have been discussing. He writes: "Our sexuality has been animalized, stripped of the intricacy of feeling with which human beings have endowed it, leaving us to contemplate only the act, and to fear our impotence in it. It is this animalization from which the sexual manuals cannot escape, even when they try to do so, because they are reflections of it. They might [as well] be textbooks for veterinarians." (Fairlie, *The Seven Deadly Sins Today*, p. 182.)

In this matter of counterfeit intimacy and deceptive gratification, I express particular caution to the men who read this message. I have heard all my life that it is the young woman who has to assume the responsibility for controlling the limits of intimacy in courtship because a young man cannot. Seldom have I heard any point made about this subject that makes me more disappointed than that. What kind of man is he, what priesthood or power or strength or self-control does this man have, that lets him develop in society, grow to the age of mature accountability, perhaps even pursue a university education and prepare to affect the future of colleagues and kingdoms and the course of the world, yet he does not have the mental capacity or the moral will to say, "I will not do that thing"? No, this sorry drugstore psychology would have us say, "I just can't help myself. My glands have complete control over my life—my mind, my will, my entire future."

To say that a young woman in such a relationship has to bear her responsibility and that of the young man too is one of the most inappropriate suggestions I can imagine. In most instances if there is sexual transgression, I lay the burden squarely on the shoulders of the young man—for our purposes probably a priesthood bearer—and that's where I believe God intended responsibility to be. In saying that, I do not excuse young women who exercise no restraint and have not the character or conviction to demand intimacy only in its rightful role. I have had enough experience in Church callings to know that women as well as men can be predatory. But I also refuse to accept the feigned innocence of some young man who wants to sin and calls it psychology.

Indeed, most tragically, it is the young woman who is most often the victim; it is the young woman who most often suffers the greater pain; it is the young woman who most often feels used and abused and terribly unclean. And for that imposed uncleanliness a man will pay, as surely as the sun sets and rivers run to the sea.

Note the prophet Jacob's straightforward language on this account in the Book of Mormon. After a bold confrontation on the subject of sexual transgression among the Nephites, he quotes Jehovah: "For behold, I, the Lord, have seen the sorrow, and heard the mourning of the *daughters* of my people in the land. . . . And I will not suffer, saith the Lord of Hosts, that the cries of the fair *daughters* of this people . . . shall come up unto me against the *men* of my people, saith the Lord of Hosts.

"For they shall not lead away captive the *daughters* of my people because of their tenderness, save I shall visit them with a sore curse, even unto destruction." (Jacob 2:31-34. Italics added.)

Don't be deceived and don't be destroyed. Unless such fire is controlled, your clothes and your future will be burned, and your world, short of painful and perfect repentance, will go up in flames. I give that to you on good word: I give it to you on God's word.

Third, after soul and symbol comes the word sacrament, *a term closely related to the other two.*

Sexual intimacy is not only a symbolic union between a man and a woman — the uniting of their very souls — but it is also symbolic of a union between mortals and deity, between otherwise ordinary and fallible humans uniting for a rare and special moment with God himself and all the powers by which he gives life in this wide universe of ours.

In this latter sense, human intimacy is a sacrament, a very special kind of symbol. For our purpose, a sacrament could be any one of a number of gestures or acts or ordinances that unite us with God and his limitless powers. We are imperfect and mortal; he is perfect and immortal. But from time to time — indeed, as often as is possible and appropriate — we find ways and go to places and create circumstances where we can unite symbolically with him and, in so doing, gain access to his power. Those special moments of union with God are sacramental moments, such as kneeling at a marriage altar, or blessing a newborn baby, or partaking of the emblems of the Lord's Supper. This latter ordinance is the one we in the Church have come to associate most traditionally with the word *sacrament,* though it is technically only one of many such moments when we formally take the hand of God and feel his divine power.

These are moments when we quite literally unite our will with God's will, our spirit with his spirit, where communion through the veil becomes very real. At such moments we not only acknowledge his divinity, but we also quite literally take something of that divinity to ourselves. Such are the holy sacraments.

Now, I know of no one who would rush into a sacramental service, grab the linen from the tables, throw the bread the full length of the room, tip the water trays onto the floor, and laughingly retreat from the building to await an opportunity to do the same thing at another worship service the next Sunday. No one would do that during one of the truly sacred moments of our religious worship. Nor would anyone violate any of the other sacramental moments in our lives, those times when we consciously claim God's power and by invitation stand with him in privilege and principality.

But I wish to stress, as my third of three reasons to be clean, that sexual union is also, in its own profound way, a very real sacrament of the highest order, a union not only of a man and a woman but very much the union of that man and that woman with God. Indeed, if our definition of sacrament is that act of claiming and sharing and exercising God's own inestimable power, then I know of virtually no other divine privilege so routinely given to us all—women or men, ordained or unordained, Latter-day Saint or non-Latter-day Saint—than the miraculous and majestic power of transmitting life, the unspeakable, unfathomable, unbroken power of procreation. There are those special moments in our lives when the other, more formal ordinances of the gospel—the sacraments, if you will—allow us to feel the grace and grandeur of God's power. Many are one-time experiences (such as our own confirmation or our own marriage), and some are repeatable (such as administering to the sick or doing ordinance work for others in the temple). But I know of nothing so earth-shatteringly powerful and yet so universally and unstintingly given to us as the God-given power available in every one of us from our early teen years on to create a human body, that wonder of all wonders, a genetically and spiritually unique being never before seen in the history of the world and never to be duplicated again in all the ages of eternity: a child, *our* child—with eyes and ears and fingers and toes and a future of unspeakable grandeur.

Imagine that, if you will. Veritable teenagers—and all of us for many decades thereafter—carrying daily, hourly, minute-to-minute, virtually every waking and sleeping moment of our lives, the power and the chemistry and the eternally transmitted seeds of life to grant someone else her second estate, someone else his next level of development in the divine plan of salvation. I submit to you that no power, priesthood or otherwise, is given by God so universally to so many with virtually no control over its use except *self*-control. And I submit that we will never be more like God at any other time in this life than when we are expressing that particular power. Of all the titles he has chosen for himself, Father is the one he declares, and creation is his watchword—especially human creation, creation in his image. His glory isn't a mountain, as stunning as mountains are. It isn't in sea or sky or snow or sunrise, as beautiful as they all are. It isn't in art or technology, be that a concerto or computer. No, his glory—and his grief—is in his children. We—you and I—are his prized possessions, and we are the earthly evidence, however inadequate, of what he truly is. Human life is the greatest of God's powers, the most mysterious and magnificent chem-

195

istry of it all, and you and I have been given it, but under the most serious and sacred of restrictions. You and I—who can make neither mountain nor moonlight, not one raindrop or a single rose—have this greater gift in an absolutely unlimited way. And the only control placed on us is self-control—self-control born of respect for the divine sacramental power it is.

Surely God's trust in us to respect this future-forming gift is an awesomely staggering one. We who may not be able to repair a bicycle or assemble an average jigsaw puzzle can yet, in all of our weaknesses and imperfections, carry this procreative power which makes us so very much like God in at least that one grand and majestic way.

Souls. Symbols. Sacraments. Do these words suggest why human intimacy is such a serious matter? Why it is so right and rewarding and stunningly beautiful when it is within marriage and approved of God (not just "good" but "*very* good," he declared to Adam and Eve), and so blasphemously wrong—like unto murder—when it is outside such a covenant? It is my understanding that we park and pet and sleep over and sleep with at the peril of our very lives. Our penalty may not come on the precise day of our transgression, but it comes surely and certainly enough, and were it not for a merciful God and the treasured privilege of personal repentance, far too many would even now be feeling that hellish pain which, like the passion we have been discussing, is also always described in the metaphor of fire. Someday, somewhere, sometime the morally unclean will, until they repent, pray like the rich man, wishing Lazarus to "dip . . . his finger in the water and cool my tongue; for I am tormented in this flame." (Luke 16:24.)

In closing, consider this from two students of civilization's long, instructive story:

"No one man [or woman], however brilliant or well-informed, can come in one lifetime to such fullness of understanding as to safely judge and dismiss the customs or institutions of his society, for these are the wisdom of generations after centuries of experiment in the laboratory of history. A youth boiling with hormones will wonder why he should not give full freedom to his sexual desires; and if he is unchecked by custom, morals, or laws, he may ruin his life [or hers] before he matures sufficiently to understand that sex is a river of fire that must be banked and cooled by a hundred restraints if it is not to consume in chaos both the individual and the group." (Will and Ariel Durant, *The Lessons of History* [New York: Simon & Schuster, 1968], pp. 35-36.)

Or, in the more ecclesiastical words of James E. Talmage:

"It has been declared in the solemn word of revelation, that the spirit and the body constitute the soul of man; and, therefore, we should look upon this body as something that shall endure in the resurrected state, beyond the grave, something to be kept pure and holy. Be not afraid of soiling its hands; be not afraid of scars that may come to it if won in earnest effort, or [won] in honest fight, but beware of scars that disfigure, that have come to you in places where you ought not have gone, that have befallen you in unworthy undertakings [pursued where you ought not have been]; beware of the wounds of battles in which you have been fighting on the wrong side." *(Conference Report,* October 1913, p. 117.)

If some are feeling the "scars . . . that have come to you in places where you ought not have gone," to them is extended the special peace and promise available through the atoning sacrifice of the Lord Jesus Christ. His love and the restored gospel principles and ordinances that make that love available to us with all their cleansing and healing power are freely given. The power of these principles and ordinances, including complete and redeeming repentance, are fully realized only in this, the true and living church of the true and living God. We should all "come unto Christ" for the fullness of soul and symbol and sacrament he offers us.

Chapter 17

I STAND ALL AMAZED

Surely the reason Christ said on the cross, "Father, forgive them," was because even in that terribly trying hour, he knew this was the message he had come through all eternity to deliver. The entire plan of salvation would have been lost had he withdrawn his forgiveness extended to the whole human family. It is the quintessential moment of his ministry, as perfect in its example as it was painful to endure.

One of our favorite hymns begins with the words "I stand all amazed." (*Hymns*, 1985, no. 193.) In any consideration of Christ's life, surely there is reason to be amazed in every way. We are amazed at his premortal role as the great Jehovah, agent of his Father, creator of the earth, guardian of the entire family of man. We are amazed at his coming to earth and the circumstances surrounding his advent, following millennia of revelatory leadership to Adam and Abraham and Moses and Lehi and all the prophets of old. We are amazed by his good and humble stepfather and by the young virgin who was his earthly mother. We are amazed at the miracle of his conception. We are amazed at the poverty of his birth and the loneliness of it, which would only be a prefiguration of all the loneliness to come.

We are amazed that at only twelve years of age he was already about his Father's business, sitting in the midst of the doctors of the law where "they were hearing him, and asking him questions" (JST Luke 2:46). We are amazed at the formal initiation of his ministry, his baptism and spiritual gifts, and the calling of very ordinary men to stand with him in teaching what would be extraordinary and often very unpopular doctrines. We are amazed that everywhere he went, the forces of evil went before him, and that they knew him from the beginning, even if mortals did not. At the same time that some were saying, "Is not this Jesus, the son of Joseph, whose father and mother we know?" (John 6:42), the devils were calling out, "Let us alone; what have we to do with thee, thou Jesus of Nazareth? art thou come to destroy us? [We] know thee who thou art: the Holy One of God" (Luke 4:34).

We stand all amazed as these forces of evil were cast out and retreated and defeated, even as the lame were made to walk, the blind to see, the deaf to hear, the infirm to stand. Indeed, we are all amazed at every movement and moment— as every generation from Adam to the end of the world must be.

But for me there is no greater amazement and no more difficult personal challenge than when, after the anguish in Gethsemane, after being mocked, beaten, and scourged, Jesus staggers under his load at the crest of Calvary and says, "Father, forgive them; for they know not what they do." (Luke 23:34.)

If ever there is a moment when I indeed stand all amazed, it is here, for this is an amazement of a different kind. So much of the mystery of his power and ministry tear at my mind. The circumstances of his birth, the breadth and variety of his ministry and miracles, the self-summoned power of the resurrection: before all of these I stand all amazed and say, "How did he do it?" But here with disciples who abandoned him in his hour of greatest need, here fainting under the weight of his cross and the sins of all mankind that were attached to it, here rent by piercing spikes in his palms and in his wrists and in his feet—here now the amazement tears not at my *mind* but at my *heart*, and I ask not *"How* did he do it" but "*Why* did he do it?" It is here that I examine my life, not against the miraculousness of his, but against the mercifulness of it, and it is here that I find how truly short I fall in emulation of the Master.

For me, this is a higher order of amazement. I am startled enough by his ability to heal the sick and raise the dead, but I have had something of that experience in a limited way, as many have as well. We are lesser vessels and undoubtedly unworthy of the privilege, but we have seen the miracles of the Lord repeated in our own lives and in our own homes and with our own portion of the priesthood. But mercy? Forgiveness? Atonement? Reconciliation? Too often, that is a different matter.

How could he forgive his tormenters at that moment? With all that pain, with blood having fallen from every pore, surely he doesn't need to be thinking of others *now*, does he? Surely he doesn't need to think of others every minute all the time, and especially not with this pack of jackals who are laughing and spitting, stripping him of his clothing and his rights and his dignity. Or is this yet one more amazing evidence that he really was perfect and intends us to be also? Is it only coincidental—or absolutely intentional—that in the Sermon on the Mount, as something of a last requirement before stating perfection as our goal, he reminds us, "Love your enemies, bless them that curse you, do good to them that hate you, and pray for them which despitefully use you, and persecute you"? (Matthew 5:44.)

I'd rather raise the dead. I'd rather restore sight and steady a palsied hand. I'd rather do anything than to love my enemies and forgive those who hurt me or my children or my children's children, and especially those who laugh and delight in the brutality of it.

"And when [Pilate] had scourged Jesus, he delivered him to be crucified. Then the soldiers of the governor took Jesus into the common hall, and gathered unto him the whole band of soldiers. And they stripped him, and put on him a scarlet robe. And when they had platted a crown of thorns, they put it upon his head, and a reed in his right hand: and they bowed the knee before him, and mocked him, saying, Hail, King of the Jews! And they spit upon him, and took the reed, and smote him on the head. And after that they had mocked him, they took the robe off from him, and put his own raiment on him, and led him away to crucify him." (Matthew 27:26-31.)

"Father, forgive them; for they know not what they do." Who cares whether or not they know what they are doing! This is cruel and barbaric and insulting injustice to the purest and only perfect life ever lived. Here is the one person in all the world from Adam to this present hour who deserves adoration and respect and admiration and love. He deserves it because "there was no other good enough / To pay the price of sin. / He only could unlock the gate / Of heav'n and let us in." ("There Is a Green Hill Far Away," *Hymns*, 1985, no. 194.) And this is what he gets for it?

Is there no justice? Shouldn't he cry out, "Be gone with you!" as he did to those other devils? Shouldn't he condemn them all and call down the legions of angels that were always waiting at his very command?

Every generation in every dispensation of the world has had its own multitudes crowding around that cross, laughing and jeering, breaking commandments and abusing covenants. It isn't just a relative handful in the meridian of time who are guilty. It is most of the people, most of the places, most of the time, including all of us who should have known better.

What is there that makes him do it, and what lesson is there in it for us? We must go back to the beginning.

Following Adam and Eve's experience in the Garden of Eden, and their eventual expulsion from it, "Adam began to till the earth, and to have dominion over all the beasts of the field, and to eat his bread by the sweat of his brow, as I the Lord had commanded him. And Eve, also, his wife, did labor with him. . . .

"And Adam and Eve, his wife, called upon the name of

the Lord, and they heard the voice of the Lord from the way toward the Garden of Eden, speaking unto them, and they saw him not; for they were shut out from his presence. And he gave unto them commandments, that they should worship the Lord their God, and should offer the firstlings of their flocks, for an offering unto the Lord. And Adam was obedient unto the commandments of the Lord.

"And after many days an angel of the Lord appeared unto Adam, saying: Why dost thou offer sacrifices unto the Lord? And Adam said unto him: I know not, save the Lord commanded me.

"And then the angel spake, saying: This thing is a similitude of the sacrifice of the Only Begotten of the Father, which is full of grace and truth. Wherefore, thou shalt do all that thou doest in the name of the Son, and thou shalt repent and call upon God in the name of the Son forevermore." (Moses 5:1, 4-8.)

Call upon God for what? What is the nature of this first instruction to the human family? Why are they to call upon God? Is this a social visit? Is it a friendly neighborhood chat. No, this is a call for help from the lone and dreary world. This is a call from the brink of despair. "Thou shalt repent and call upon God in the name of the Son forevermore." This is a call from the personal prison of a sinful heart. It is a call for the forgiveness of sins.

And so the God and Father of us all established with those first parents in the first generation of time certain principles and ordinances fashioned to convey how such forgiveness of sins would come. Along with all else of meaning and substance in our lives, it would come through the sacrifice and example of his Only Begotten Son, who is full of grace and truth.

To serve as a constant reminder of the humiliation and suffering the Son would pay to ransom us, to serve as a constant reminder that he would not open his mouth and would be brought as a lamb to the slaughter (see Mosiah 14:7), to serve as a constant reminder of the meekness and mercy and gentleness—yes, the forgiveness—that was to mark every Christian life: for all these reasons and more, those firstborn lambs, clean and unblemished, perfect in every way, were offered on those stone altars year after and year and generation after generation, pointing us toward the great Lamb of God, his Only Begotten Son, his Firstborn, perfect and without blemish.

In offering our symbolic but much more modest sacrifice in whatever dispensation—that which reflects our broken heart and contrite spirit (see D&C 59:8)—we promise to "always remember him and keep his commandments; . . . that [we] may always have his spirit to be with [us]." (D&C 20:77.) The symbols of his sacrifice, in Adam's day or our own, were intended to help us remember to live peacefully and obediently and mercifully. And, as a result of these ordinances, it was intended that we demonstrate the gospel of Jesus Christ in our long-suffering and human kindness one for another, as he demonstrated it for us on that cross.

But over the centuries it seems never to have worked that way—at least not often enough. Cain quickly managed to get it wrong. As the Prophet Joseph Smith noted: "God . . . prepared a sacrifice in the gift of His own Son who should be sent in due time, to prepare a way, or open a door through which man might enter into the Lord's presence, whence he had been cast out for disobedience. . . . By faith in this atonement or plan of redemption, Abel offered to God a sacrifice that was accepted, which was the firstlings of the flock. Cain offered of the fruit of the ground, and was not accepted, because he . . . could not exercise faith contrary to the plan of heaven. It must be shedding the blood of the Only Begotten to atone for man; for this was the plan of redemption, and without the shedding of blood was no remission; and as the sacrifice was instituted for a type, by which man was to discern the great Sacrifice which God had prepared; to offer a sacrifice contrary to that, no faith could be exercised, because re-

203

demption was not purchased in that way, nor the power of the atonement instituted after that order. . . . Certainly, the shedding of the blood of a beast could be beneficial to no man, except it was done in imitation, or as a type, or explanation of what was to be offered through the gift of God Himself; and this performance done with an eye looking forward in faith on the power of that great Sacrifice for a remission of sins." (*History of the Church* 2:15-16.)

And so others of us in every age and season, a little Cain-like, would come home fresh from morning oblations to scream at a spouse, devastate a child, kick the dog, or merely lie a little, cheat a little, and dig a pit for the neighbor. The attention span we've shown in relation to our saving ordinances over the dispensations would by comparison make preschoolers look like college graduates. Too often we have forgotten *why* even before the blood was dry on the altar or the trays were returned to the table or the robes of the holy priesthood folded and put away for yet another session.

Saul, king in Israel, demonstrated the problem. In explicit contradiction to the Lord's instructions, he brought back from the Amalekites "the best of the sheep and of the oxen: to sacrifice unto the Lord [his] God." Samuel, in utter anguish, cried: "Hath the Lord as great delight in burnt offerings and sacrifice, as in obeying the voice of the Lord? Behold, to obey is better than sacrifice, and to hearken than the fat of rams. For rebellion is as the sin of witchcraft, and stubbornness is as iniquity and idolatry. Because thou hast rejected the word of the Lord, he hath also rejected thee from being king." (1 Samuel 15:15, 22-23.)

Why is rebellion (or stubbornness or disobedience in our ordinances) like witchcraft? Because it makes a statement about our loyalty and our understanding of what God is really like and what he really wants. Saul, who understood the method but not the meaning of his sacrifice, and the Latter-day Saint who faithfully goes to sacrament meeting but is no more merciful or patient or forgiving as a result—both are much the same as the witch and the idolater. They go through the motions of the ordinances without loyalty to or understanding of the reasons for which these ordinances were established—obedience, gentleness, and loving kindness in the search for forgiveness of our sins.

Ordinances pursued in error and altered in meaning mark an apostate priesthood and an idolatrous nation. As the Prophet Joseph taught us, we can rest assured that God was not interested in the death of innocent little animals—*unless* the meaning of those altars truly alters the nature of our lives.

At one particularly low point in Israelite history, the Lord cried out to his children: "I hate, I despise your feast days. . . . Though ye offer me burnt offerings and your meat offerings, I will not accept them: neither will I regard the peace offerings of your fat beasts. Take thou away from me the noise of thy songs; for I will not hear the melody of thy viols. But let judgment run down as waters, and righteousness as a mighty stream." (Amos 5:21-24.)

And so it was so much of the time until we come to this final parable:

"There was a certain householder, which planted a vineyard, and hedged it round about, and digged a winepress in it, and built a tower, and let it out to husbandmen, and went into a far country: and when the time of the fruit drew near, he sent his servants to the husbandmen, that they might receive the fruits of it. And the husbandmen took his servants, and beat one, and killed another, and stoned another.

"Again, he sent other servants more than the first: and they did unto them likewise. But last of all he sent unto them his son, saying, They will reverence my son.

"But when the husbandmen saw the son, they said among themselves, This is the heir; come, let us kill him, and let us seize on his inheritance. And they caught him, and cast him out of the vineyard, and slew him." (Matthew 21:33-39.)

That is the moment at which we find ourselves on the summit of Golgotha. It is not a pleasant story. Through patience that seems inordinately generous, the Father and the Son have waited and watched and worked in this vineyard for mercy to run down as waters, and righteousness as a mighty stream. But mercy and righteousness have not run. Not only have the prophets and faithful few been killed, but now so is to be the son of the Lord of the vineyard. A terrible, incalculable price is to be paid, and it wounds the human heart to tell it.

In the midst of the swearing and the spit, the thorns and the threats, the ridicule and the rending of his garments; added to the crushing weight of his own body straining for support on the very nails that have been driven into his hands and into his feet; and with friends in retreat and foes as far as the eye could see—the unexpected happens, the worst possible scene in this divine drama unfolds.

Perhaps the briefest glimpse is given of the terrible emotions and forces at work here when we read lines intentionally preserved for us in the original Aramaic: "Eli, Eli, lama sabachthani? that is to say, My God, my God, why hast thou forsaken me?" (Matthew 27:46.)

There is one thing and one thing alone this Only Begotten Son has been sure of: the love and companionship and unwavering support of his Father. Consider these lines taken almost at random from the Gospel of John. They are suggestive of a theme that runs throughout that book.

"The Son can do nothing of himself, but what he seeth the Father do: . . . For the Father loveth the Son, and sheweth him all things that himself doeth." (John 5:19-20.)

"I came down from heaven, not to do mine own will, but the will of him that sent me." (John 6:38.)

"I am not come of myself, but he that sent me is true, whom ye know not. But I know him." (John 7:28-29.)

"The Father that sent me beareth witness of me. . . . If ye had known me, ye should have known my Father also." (John 8:18-19.)

206

"He gave me a commandment, what I should say, and what I should speak." (John 12:49.)

"Behold, the hour cometh, yea, is now come, that ye shall be scattered, every man to his own, and shall leave me alone: and yet I am not alone, because the Father is with me." (John 16:32.)

And then this assertion, perhaps the most painful of all: "I am not alone, but I and the Father that sent me. . . . He that sent me is with me: the Father hath not left me alone; for I do always those things that please him." (John 8:16, 29.)

That one constant thread of doctrine and belief, the one certainty he had in spite of what might happen among mortal friend and foe: "[My] Father hath not left me alone; for I do always those things which please him."

And now, "Eli, Eli, lama sabachthani? . . . My God, my God, why hast thou forsaken me."

May I share this from Elder Melvin J. Ballard, written many years ago.

"I ask you, what father and mother could stand by and listen to the cry of their children in distress . . . and not render assistance? I have heard of mothers throwing themselves into raging streams when they could not swim a stroke to save their drowning children, [I have heard of fathers] rushing into burning buildings [at the peril of their own lives] to rescue those whom they loved.

"We cannot stand by and listen to those cries without it touching our hearts. . . . He had the power to save and He loved His Son, and He could have saved Him. He might have rescued Him from the insult of the crowds. He might have rescued Him when the crown of thorns was placed upon His head. He might have rescued Him when the Son, hanging between two thieves, was mocked with, 'Save thyself, and come down from the cross. He saved others; himself he cannot save.' He listened to all this. He saw that Son condemned; He saw Him drag the cross through the streets of Jerusalem and faint under its load. He saw the Son finally upon Calvary;

He saw His body stretched out upon the wooden cross; He saw the cruel nails driven through hands and feet, and the blows that broke the skin, tore the flesh, and let out the life's blood of His [Only Begotten] Son. . . .

"[He] looked on [all that] with great grief and agony over His Beloved [Child], until there seems to have come a moment when even our Saviour cried out in despair: 'My God, my God, why hast thou forsaken me.'

"In that hour I think I can see our dear Father behind the veil looking upon these dying struggles, . . . His great heart almost breaking for the love that He had for His Son. Oh, in that moment when He might have saved His Son, I thank Him and praise Him that He did not fail us. . . . I rejoice that He did not interfere, and that His love for us made it possible for Him to endure to look upon the sufferings of His [Only Begotten] and give Him finally to us, our Saviour and our Redeemer. Without Him, without His sacrifice, we would have remained, and we would never have come glorified into His presence. . . .

"This is what it cost, in part, for our Father in heaven to give the gift of His Son unto men. . . .

"Our God is a jealous God—jealous lest we should [ever] ignore or forget and slight his greatest gift unto us"—the life of his Firstborn Son. (*Melvin J. Ballard, Crusader for Righteousness* [Salt Lake City: Bookcraft, 1966], pp. 136-38.)

So how do we make sure that we never "ignore or slight or forget" his greatest of all gifts unto us?

We do so by showing our desire for a remission of our sins and our eternal gratitude for that most courageous of all prayers, "Father, forgive them; for they know not what they do." (Luke 23:34.) We do so by joining in the work of forgiving sins.

" 'Bear ye one another's burdens, and so fulfil the law of Christ,' [Paul commands us]. (Gal. 6:2) . . . The law of Christ, which it is our duty to fulfil, is the bearing of the cross. My brother's burden which I must bear is not only his outward lot [and circumstance], . . . but quite literally his sin. And the only way to bear that sin is by forgiving it in the power of the cross of Christ in which [we] now share. Thus the call to follow Christ always means a call to share [in] the work of forgiving men their sins. Forgiveness is the Christlike suffering which it is the Christian's duty to bear." (Dietrich Bonhoeffer, *The Cost of Discipleship*, 2nd ed. [New York: Macmillan, 1959], p. 100.)

Surely the reason Christ said, "Father, forgive them" was because even in the weakened and terribly trying hour he faced, he knew that this was the message he had come through all eternity to deliver. All of the meaning and all of the majesty of all those dispensations—indeed, the entire plan of salvation—would have been lost had he forgotten that not *in spite* of injustice and brutality and unkindness and disobedience but precisely *because* of them had he come to extend forgiveness to the family of man. Anyone can be pleasant and patient and forgiving on a good day. A Christian has to be pleasant and patient and forgiving on all days. It was the quintessential moment of Christ's ministry, and as perfect in its example as it was difficult to endure.

Is there someone who perhaps needs forgiveness? Is there someone in our home, someone in our family, someone in our neighborhood who has done an unjust or an unkind or an unchristian thing? All of us are guilty of such transgressions, so there surely must be someone who yet needs our forgiveness.

And please don't ask if that's fair—if the injured should have to bear the burden of forgiveness for the offender. Don't ask if "justice" doesn't demand that it be the other way around. No, whatever we do, we must not ask for justice. We know that what we plead for is mercy—and that is what we must be willing to give.

Can we see the tragic and ultimate irony of not granting to others what we need so badly ourselves? Perhaps the highest and holiest and purest act of cleansing would be to say in the face of unkindness and injustice that we do yet more truly love our enemies and bless them that curse us, do good to them that hate us, and pray for them that despitefully use us, and persecute us. That is the demanding pathway of perfection.

A marvelous Scottish minister once wrote:

"No man who will not forgive his neighbor, can believe that God is willing, yea wanting, to forgive him. . . . If God said, 'I forgive you' to a man who hated his brother, and if (as impossible) that voice of forgiveness should reach the man, what would it mean to him? How would the man interpret it? Would it not mean to him, 'You may go on hating. I do not mind it. You have had great provocation and are justified in your hate'?

"No doubt God takes what wrong there is, and what provocation there is, into the account: but the more provocation, the more excuse that can be urged for the hate, the more reason . . . that the hater should [forgive, and] be delivered from the hell of his [anger]." (*George MacDonald, An Anthology*, ed. C. S. Lewis [New York: Macmillan, 1947], pp. 6-7.)

I recall several years ago seeing a drama enacted at the Salt Lake airport. On this particular day, as I got off an airplane and walked into the terminal, it was immediately obvious that a missionary was coming home because the whole airport was astir with conspicuous-looking missionary friends and missionary relatives.

I tried to pick out the immediate family members. There was a father who did not look particularly comfortable in an awkward-fitting and slightly out-of-fashion suit. He seemed to be a man of the soil, with a suntan and large, work-scarred hands. His white shirt was a little frayed and was probably never worn except on Sunday.

There was a mother who was quite thin, looking as if she had worked very hard in her life. She had in her hand a handkerchief—and I think it must have been a linen handkerchief once but now it looked like tissue. It was absolutely shredded from the anticipation only the mother of a returning missionary could know.

There was a beautiful girl who—well, you know about girls and returning missionaries. She appeared to be on the verge of cardiac arrest. I thought that if the young man didn't come soon, she would not make it without some oxygen.

Two or three younger brothers and sisters were running around, largely oblivious to the scene that was unfolding.

I walked past them all and started for the front of the terminal. Then I thought to myself, "This is one of the special human dramas in our lives. Stick around and enjoy it." So I stopped. I slipped into the back of the crowd to wait and watch. The missionaries were starting to come off the plane.

I found myself starting to guess as to who would make the break first. I thought probably the girlfriend would want to most of all, but undoubtedly she was struggling with discretion. Two years is a long time, you know, and maybe one shouldn't appear too assertive. Then a look at that handkerchief convinced me that the mother was probably the one. She obviously needed to hold something, so the child she had carried and nurtured and gone down into the valley of the shadow of death to deliver would be just what the doctor ordered. Or perhaps it would be the boisterous little brother—if he happened to look up long enough to know the plane was in.

As I sat there weighing these options, I saw the missionary start to come down the stairs. I knew he was the one by the squeal of the crowd. He looked like Captain Moroni, clean and handsome and straight. Undoubtedly he had known the sacrifice this mission had meant to his father and mother, and it had made him exactly the missionary he appeared to be. He had his hair trimmed for the trip home, his suit was worn but clean, his slightly tattered raincoat was still protecting him from the chill his mother had so often warned him about.

He came to the bottom of the steps and started out across

211

the apron toward our building and then, sure enough, somebody couldn't take it any longer. It wasn't the mother, and it wasn't the girlfriend, and it wasn't the rowdy little brother. That big, slightly awkward, quiet and bronzed giant of a man put an elbow into the ribcage of a flight attendant and ran, just simply ran, out onto that apron and swept his son into his arms.

The oxygen summoned for the girlfriend could have now been better directed toward the missionary. This big bear of a father grabbed him, took him clear off his feet, and held him for the longest time. He just held him and said nothing. The boy dropped his bag, put both arms around his dad, and they held each other very tightly. It seemed like all eternity stood still, and for a precious moment the Salt Lake City airport was the center of the entire universe. It was as if all the world had gone silent out of respect for such a sacred moment.

And then I thought of God the Eternal Father watching his boy go out to serve, to sacrifice when he didn't have to do it, paying his own way, so to speak, costing everything he had saved all his life to give. At that precious moment it was not too difficult to imagine that father speaking with some emotion to those who could hear, "This is my beloved son, in whom I am well pleased." And it was also possible to imagine that triumphant returning son, saying, "It is finished. Father, into thy hands I commend my spirit."

Now I don't know what kind of seven-league boots a father uses to rush through the space of eternity. But even in my limited imagination I can see that reunion in the heavens. And I pray for one like it for you and for me. I pray for reconciliation and for forgiveness, for mercy, and for the Christian growth and Christian character we must develop if we are to enjoy such a moment fully.

I stand all amazed that for a man like me, full of egotism and transgression and intolerance and impatience, there is a chance. But if I've heard the "good news" correctly, there is a chance — for me and for you and for everyone who is willing to keep hoping and to keep trying and to allow others the same privilege.

> I marvel that he would descend from his throne divine,
> To rescue a soul so rebellious and proud as mine. . . .
> I think of his hands pierced and bleeding to pay the debt!
> Such mercy, such love, and devotion can I forget?
> No, no, I will praise and adore at the mercy seat,
> Until at the glorified throne I kneel at his feet. . . .
> Oh, it is wonderful, wonderful to me!

INDEX

215